Designing Creative Resumes

Gregg Berryman

W9-ADM-566

Crisp Publications
1200 Hamilton Ct.
Menlo Park, CA 94025

3 2280 00553 7188

Copyright © 1990 by Crisp Publications, Inc.

All rights reserved. This book or any part
thereof may not be reproduced in any form
whatsoever, whether by graphic, visual,
electronic, filming, microfilming, tape recording
or any other means, without the prior written
permission of Crisp Publications, Inc. except in
the case of brief passages embodied in critical
reviews and articles.

ISBN 1-56052-053-1

Berryman, Gregg, 1942-
    Designing creative resumes / Gregg Berryman.
        p.   cm.
    Includes index.
    ISBN 1-56052-053-1 : $14.95
    1. Résumés (Employment)   I. Title
HF5383.B43   1991
650.14--dc20

91-21443
CIP

Contents

Acknowledgements

Dedicated to my wife Phyllis for her help and support throughout this project.

Many thanks to the creative professionals, most of them my former students, for their consent to reprint the resume samples shown in this book, to Gaylord Bennitt for the portrait illustration on the back cover, and to all the production personnel at William Kaufmann, Inc. for their patience and encouragement.

Design: Gregg Berryman
Typing: Phyllis Berryman
Editor: Ike Burke
Typography: Jonathan Peck Typographers
Film: Color Tech
Printer: Bawden Printing, Inc.
Paper: Bawden Offset White 60#
Type: American Typewriter, Helvetica

Introduction

Resumes are used by job seekers of all types to help them land or change employment. Millions of these important documents are produced annually but most have little verbal or visual impact. In fact most resumes are, to say the least, forgettable.

This book is about a special kind of resume, the creative resume. Employers of creative professionals are inevitably articulate and particular. These busy executives spend a part of every workday producing persuasive words and images. They are by nature critical and demanding. An average resume makes little impact on them. However, a creative resume will attract the attention of creative managers and provoke their response.

Your creative resume should be exceptional. It must elevate you above the crowd and clearly show that you can produce results. It should link your needs with those of a potential employer. Above all, your creative resume must stimulate the employer to meet and interview you.

Like most creative professionals, you may assemble many resumes during your career. The first might be for an internship, cooperative work experience, or summer job. Later when you seek a full-time entry-level position, the resume becomes a critical part of your job search package. Whenever you change your employment an updated resume is necessary. The resume might also be used effectively when consulting or applying for grants and fellowships.

The creative resume is a special tool. It establishes your credibility. It leaves a lasting impression. The creative resume is a crisp self advertisement, a polished mirror of you. It establishes in the mind of the employer your personal identity. The creative resume must show you as a direct benefit to the company, organization, or institution. Remember, the first thing it must do is help to get you an interview.

Resume
Contents

Resume contents will vary from one individual to another. Your data are unique. Emphasize this fact. Beware of the packaged resume produced by resume services. These have a tendency to be equalizers. The creative resume is built on individual differences rather than similarities. Strive to be concise yet distinct. Employers are interested in your unique talents.

Your creative resume need not fit any one "correct" writing style. Select a comfortable format that will effectively deliver your vital information. Arrange your data in the reverse chronological, functional, narrative or accomplishment formats. The reverse chronological plan positions your education and experience from latest to earliest. Functional arrangement disregards chronology while organizing your work experience by job title function. The narrative resume is written first person, tells a story about you, and presents data in complete sentences. Accomplishment resumes feature positive achievements and emphasize results over chronology. Sometimes a writing format that combines styles is effective. Your goal is to present a consistent, palatable document, an honest reflection of you.

Keep the creative resume brief, clear and error free. Use active, correct grammar. Don't trust yourself as the sole editor. Feedback during the preliminary writing stage will help to refine your presentation. Rely on the help of an author, copy editor, or professor to help polish rough edges. As a courtesy to your editor, be sure to prepare preliminary drafts in double-spaced typewritten form, one topic per page. To expect an editor to plow through poor handwriting or illegible handlettering, with no space for corrections is an insult. Use the constructive criticism of your editor to hone the text and rewrite it if necessary. Build your creative resume with essential information edited into an economical yet comfortable format.

achieved
analyzed
arranged

created
conducted
constructed
coordinated

delivered
designed
developed
directed

established
exhibited
evaluated

gained
generated

implemented
improved
increased

managed
motivated

narrated
negotiated

operated
organized

planned
prepared
presented
produced
promoted

realized
researched

strengthened
supervised

tested
trained

upgraded
utilized

Employment Objective

A short, to-the-point job objective is appropriate when you apply for a specific internship or position beyond entry level. If you decide to use a placement agency, the job objective is necessary to link you with potential employers. It helps target your employment more exactly. By listing Corporate Design Manager, Senior Package Designer, or Technical Illustrator as your job objective you gain priority consideration for matching job titles. Avoid multi-sentence or full paragraph job objectives. They tend to confuse the employer rather than clarify your intentions.

When seeking your first career position, treat the job objective carefully. Consider excluding it from the resume, including it instead in your cover letter where you can target a job and a specific individual.

By mentioning a job objective on your resume you may be taking yourself out of the running for some positions with real potential. The job search process often uncovers positions very different from your original target. The job objective that begins as functional information may turn into a burden on the creative resume.

Personal Information

Present clearly on the resume your name, address, and telephone number. Don't forget the zip code portion of the address. Remember that most interview appointments and other negotiations are conducted by telephone. Area code is important. Name, address and telephone number must be easy to locate with a quick visual scan.

A resume listing two telephone numbers or addresses can be confusing and annoying. Yet certain situations, like residential moves, vacations, or extended travel, may make backup information seem inviting. Ask yourself "Will a phone call to my primary address reach me the same day if I am not there to answer it?" If "Yes," then a single address and phone number is sufficient.

Keep potential employers notified by telephone or brief letter of your whereabouts. Your creative resume will have a longer working life if the address and phone number remains unchanged.

Additional personal information should be weighed carefully. Employers are prevented by law from requesting age and marital status, but if your research shows that an employer prefers younger or married employees, such data might fit in. Listing birthdate (9-15-60) is more efficient than indicating your age in years (25) because it doesn't render your resume obsolete at your next birthday. Marital status can also change quickly. Most job seekers consider themselves healthy, so this information may best be left out. Handicaps may be discussed in the interview. Omit draft status except in time of conflict.

Personal interests may give you extra dimension, particularly if they relate to your target position. Two or three personal interests, sports, or hobbies suggest real involvement. Including more items may indicate a lack of focus. When in doubt, leave personal interests out of the creative resume.

Education
Training

Education is a vital resume topic when you search for an internship, co-op position, or your initial job. It diminishes in priority as you gain significant work experience.

Your alma mater brands you with a certain identity. Alumni networks and associates of your professors will usually give you an edge in the job search. Your performance in college predicts your job performance. Educational references on the creative resume demand clarity, consistency, and strategic position.

List your educational data in reverse chronological order. This sequence insures that your latest experience is read first. Include your college degrees, with dates conferred. Group the significant courses in your major and minor emphases. Arrange the courses precisely in your order of preference. Consider which special courses felt particularly challenging and comfortable. Place these at the top of your list to suggest a work preference. Adjust the sometimes lengthy and obscure titles of academic courses to fit common professional terminology. Omit nonspecific foundation courses from the creative resume.

Some educators have a high regional, national, or international profile. Concentrated study with such an individual or faculty team may open special doors. Mention of select high-profile teachers can give your creative resume an edge.

Forget high school as a resume listing. Consider doing the same for community or junior college unless your AA Degree has unusual significance. Simple mention of the two-year institution and degree date is adequate.

When listing colleges and degree dates, include the years but omit months and days. Your creative resume will be easier to scan and digest. Anticipated graduation dates can be legitimately listed.

Extraordinary class standing or grade point average should be woven in. If only average, omit this data on the resume and save it for your interview. If you earned 50-100% of your college expenses, don't hesitate to mention this. Employers are favorably impressed by self-starting students who pay their own way.

Scholarships and fellowships earned should be listed in this or a separate category. These awards place you in select company and help you stand out, as does your command of a foreign language. Travel study programs add breadth to your educational experiences and fit the creative resume.

Seminars
Workshops

Significant extension courses, workshops, and training programs add depth to your capabilities. Seminars increase your professional exposure outside the college framework. Listed on the creative resume, they chart your desire for self-improvement. Continuing education suggests a positive growth curve. It reflects your desire to remain current with the trends and technology of the Information Age.

Mention your working knowledge of typesetting, typing, accounting, management, or business practice. These skills add to your value. Participation in photography, video, computer, and photomechanical training programs offered by industry should be noted.

Indicate that the workshops listed on your creative resume had substance. Merely attending a two-hour lecture doesn't count. A solid weekend of intense hands-on involvement does. If the workshop altered your outlook, opened new creative doors, and provided you with knowledge you can demonstrate, be sure to include it. Listings should be recent. Be ready to discuss attributes of such experiences with target employers.

AIA Conventions
AIGA Conferences
ASID Conferences
Aspen Design Conferences
Art Directors' Club Events
Business by Design Workshops
CASE Seminars
Catalyst Management Seminars
Design Management Institute Conferences
Envision Design Conferences
Friends of Calligraphy Workshops
Film Festivals
GATF Seminars
Graphic Artists' Guild Seminars
Gutenberg Expositions

IABC Conferences
ICOGRADA Conferences
IDSA Conferences
Illustrators' Workshops
Kodak Technical Seminars
Nikon Workshops
Pubmart Expositions
RIT Technical Seminars
SEGD Conferences
SIGGRAPH Conferences
Stanford Design Conferences
Stanford Publishing Conferences
UCDA Conferences
University Extension Courses
Women in Communication Conferences

Work Experience

Employment History, Work Experience, Professional Experience, Work History, Experience, and Employment are alternative headings with similar meanings. Employers carefully scrutinize your past jobs. Show the positions you have held in reverse chronological order, latest to earliest. Your present position will attract the most attention at the top of the list.

Show the date of position, job title, and employer. Include the city and state of your employer. Omit the employer street address and telephone number as trivial.

A long list of previous jobs should be edited to those of interest to the target employer. Be sure to account carefully for the four or five years preceding your job search. Remember to include military positions with a stress on promotions, leadership responsibility, and acquired skills.

Your resume for an internship or first professional position may demand lumping together summer or part-time jobs. If you ever held two or three jobs concurrently, use this fact to your advantage. Employers are impressed with the organization and energy required to juggle multiple positions. Use language and style to place short-term positions in a good light.

Volunteer and field-work experiences have a place on the creative resume as long as the work you did was clearly significant. Did your efforts affect the organization, improve a program, or increase funding? Stress that your volunteer activities required interaction with people. Show that your group achieved a well-defined goal. Cooperative efforts closely parallel the job requirements of a creative position. Employers seek team players.

Work on a political campaign might be significant in your view. Some employers will have opposite political leanings. Include partisan experiences with great caution as they may cause awkward controversy.

On the creative resume you can do more than simply list positions held. Amplify your job titles list with a tight description of special skills acquired. List your accomplishments. Use a clear, concise style. Begin sentences with action verbs that feature leadership and organizational skills. "Developed", "supervised", "designed", "created", and "managed" help to build compact sentences that portray you as a doer.

Internships
Co-ops

Internships, apprenticeships, and co-op positions differ from normal jobs. Although sometimes paid, the essence of such employment is on-the-job training. Employers recognize that interns have had exposure to the daily experiences of a studio or office. At best, co-op positions give an organization a close-up look at a potential employee under fire. Little wonder that many graduates gain their first full time jobs after positive performance in these positions.

Internships should be listed on the resume in the same style as normal jobs. In reverse chronological order show date, job title, employer, city, and state. With action verbs, detail your responsibilities, and acquired skills.

If you have held several internships, consider fitting them under a separate heading of the same name. An alternative is to integrate internships under the Work Experience heading. If you choose this approach, be sure that the position is clearly labeled as internship or co-op.

Awards
Memberships

The creative resume should include a category (or categories) to list fellowships, scholarships, memberships, exhibitions, awards, publications and productions. Your early resumes might be skeletal in these areas, but later versions will probably flesh out. Headings for these items should be logical. "Fellowships" and "Scholarships" may be paired. "Exhibitions" and "Awards" fit together, as do "Publications" and "Productions."

The fellowships and scholarships you list should have been earned in competition. Naturally more prestige is attached to grants from national organizations or professional societies. List the year of the award, its title, and its source. Including the financial value of the grant is optional, but is logical for very large dollar amounts.

Memberships have a place on the creative resume. You can show an employer that you function well as part of a group. Most positions require a similar interaction and team orientation. Your active participation in a student design, marketing, or communication club indicates a genuine professional orientation. Many national professional societies have student chapters. Regional design organizations, art directors' clubs, and advertising/marketing societies encourage student membership. Get involved and record it on your creative resume.

Social and service fraternities may have a place on the creative resume if you played an important leadership or management role. Mere membership is hardly worth listing. Sometimes the Greek names of fraternal organizations can be confusing to an employer. Yet if the employer is a sorority or fraternity alum you may get special consideration. The creative resume that stresses social activities at the expense of professional involvement is misguided.

Exhibitions and awards must be kept in perspective on the resume. National competitions are important. Local student shows are usually not, unless they have been juried by professionals and you have won an award. A one-person show of your work can be significant. List the year of the show, its title, its location, and the award you received on your creative resume.

Publications seldom appear on the resume created for an internship or first position. On later resumes, evidence of your published writing or visual work may be expected or even required. Publication in a student magazine or local newspaper doesn't count for much. Significant publication in a professional magazine, annual, or journal should be listed. Indicate date, publication, title of piece, and perhaps a brief description if the title is obscure. Have a tear sheet or photocopy in your portfolio.

Productions may advance your cause if your creative resume is slanted toward computer graphics, audio-visual, film, or video. Your graduate thesis production qualifies. Date, production, title, credits, and a brief description of the piece are appropriate. Be prepared to show an employer any productions you've listed.

References

While in college you are developing resume references among the professors you impress with your performance. References may also come from the supervisor on your part-time job or the professional you work with in your internship position. Three strong references are enough.

Be sure to ask permission to use a reference's name. Confirm the address and telephone number you list. Some positions require written reference letters, but most do not. Virtually all contact between employer and reference is by telephone, so include a home phone number as a backup. Employers may become frustrated if they cannot easily reach people you've listed as references. Keep track of your references; know when they'll be traveling or on vacation.

Reference listings should be kept discrete on the creative resume. A simple statement like "References furnished upon request" is sufficient. Back up this listing with a separate sheet or card containing complete reference data. Match the type style and paper color to your resume. Keep these separate reference pieces handy for interviews or mailing.

Do not list the names, addresses, and telephone numbers of your references on your resume. Extraneous calls may invade the privacy of your references. You may want to make a change in references due to a move, sabbatical leave, position change, or even a death. Also, high-powered references can distract an employer from the focus of the resume - you. By cultivating them and tracking them well, you can make your references valuable tools in your job search. A strong reference base is essential to the creative resume.

Resume Design

A maximum design effort separates the creative resume from common fact sheets. Resume design is often overlooked or undervalued by otherwise well-prepared job seekers. Treat it like any important design task. Work at the top of your ability. Push the leading edge of your creativity. Since the resume is often your last creative piece before you accept a new position, strive to make it your best effort.

Consider how your resume will be received, handled, and stored by a potential employer. When delivered by hand, it must establish a quick positive impression. An employer often scans your resume during the interview. Critical information must be clear and easy to locate.

If you intend to mail your resume to a potential employer, think of it as a package begging to be opened. Design it for folding if you want it to arrive in a business-size envelope. To avoid a crushed, bent, or dimpled look, ship it in a rigid envelope, box, or mailing tube. Make a strong visual impression with the mailed resume to insure that it reaches your specific target employer. Avoid giving your resume package the appearance of junk mail. You don't want it to be dropped in the round file without being read.

Pay attention to mailing details. Address the envelope to a specific person in the target firm. Include their job title. Type rather than hand letter. Match the type style of your cover letter if that is to be included in the package. Remember to supply your current return address. Select postage stamps rather than use a postal meter. Consider well-designed commemoratives that reflect your visual sensitivity and complement the envelope color. Rubber stamp the package with "First Class Mail," "Priority Mail," or "Do Not Bend," as appropriate. Above all make the package appear to contain the important business that it does - your resume.

Resumes are most often stored in files with letters and other documents. In corporations and job-placement firms, active files contain hundreds or even thousands of resumes. Design your creative resume to fit common storage systems; otherwise it may be excluded from the file.

Virtually all resumes are designed to the 8-1/2 x 11 inch format. If you need more space for resume contents add additional pages by folding. Avoid sizes and shapes that extend outside the edges of file folders. Even if your odd-sized resume manages to get filed, it will probably wind up with tattered edges. Smaller resume sizes easily fit filing systems but are difficult to retrieve and may get buried inside. Strive to design your resume so well that it will be tacked to the wall or bulletin board by employers.

Resume
Design

Once you understand how your resume is likely to be received, handled, and stored, your design task begins. The resume's essence is your unique information. Write, rewrite, and edit your resume's contents; then organize the resulting data. Prioritize the information. Explore positions on the format page that the employer will find logical. Make sure that all important facts can be picked up in a brief scan. Most obvious should be your name, address, and telephone number. Arrange the Education, Experience, Personal, Awards, and Membership information blocks to fit your unique profile. Your ability to organize information on the creative resume will make a strong impression on employers.

Type size is an important design consideration. Whether you choose to typewrite or typeset the resume, beware of selecting extremely small type. Consider reducing typewriter type twenty to twenty-five percent to produce a size comparable to body typefaces. Full-size typewriter type consumes excessive space and may require additional resume pages. Most employers will find 8-, 9-, and 10-point body typesetting comfortable to read.

Your creative resume should blend form and content in a unique manner. It should convey your design philosophy and career direction. If your goal is publication design, the resume might take on a vertical, editorial look, stressing columns and complementary heads. An advertising resume might resemble a full page ad with stress on a creative headline and an integrated photo or illustration. A calligrapher might blend elegant hand-lettered headlines with appropriate body type. If you seek a corporate design position, perhaps treat the resume as an annual report page with chronology and graphs. A copy editor might develop a resume resembling a manuscript, complete with proofreader marks.

A strong concept is the foundation of your creative resume. It can help overcome rather ordinary data. Powerful, direct communication is necessary. Try out your ideas on friends in brainstorming sessions. Work closely with a teacher or creative professional to develop design directions. Ask for feedback while you refine your strongest concept. Handle your final resume idea with finesse. Remember that the distance between the appropriate and the absurd is often quite short.

Each creative resume will take a unique visual direction. The resume's visual appearance should mirror your creativity. As the information content of the resume reflects your personal history, its visual content predicts your job future.

Thumbnails

Thumbnail sketches help you to think on paper. You transform ideas into visual reality with these structured doodles. Thumbnail techniques are easy to master and are useful for developing the creative resume. These idea sketches are small but in proportion to the printed piece. If your resume is 8-1/2 x 11 inches, your thumbnails might be one quarter, one third, or one half that size. Try some at each size to explore the visualizing format that feels most comfortable to you.

The reduced size of thumbnail sketches allows you to create many in a short time. Each sketch should take but a few minutes to complete. Think in color, using your pencils, pens, and markers. Produce lots of ideas. Don't crowd them on the sheet. Allow each sketch to "breathe", with ample surrounding space on the page. Empty your brain. Never reject an idea until you test it thoroughly with sketches.

Small sketches have an advantage. They don't involve detail that might interfere with your resume idea. Type can be indicated quickly with simple lines. You can experiment with a variety of type formats, composition systems and layouts. To speed development of the most promising thumbnails, trace over them. Design and refine as you repeat the tracing process to develop your creative resume.

Most significant graphic design doesn't happen by hit or miss. Communication excellence usually results from the development of visual alternatives. Thumbnail techniques help you refine your ideas. Keep your resume sketch size and style consistent so you will be able to compare your sketches. Tack the sketches on the wall side by side. Your best ideas will certainly emerge. Invite critical feedback from others at this stage in the process.

How many thumbnails should you do? Certainly more than a few. Give yourself the chance to explore several ideas. Use the tracing process to develop your creative resume. A unique resume layout will probably not emerge immediately. Be patient! Devote a little time and effort to the task. Flow with the process. Soon an original mini-resume will appear. While moderate in scope, the creative resume is certainly one of the most important design problems you will ever solve.

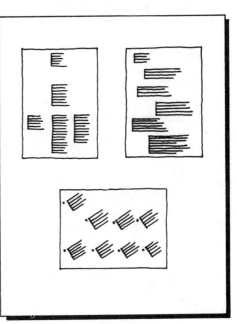

Thumbnails

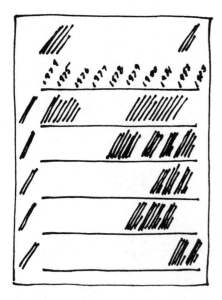

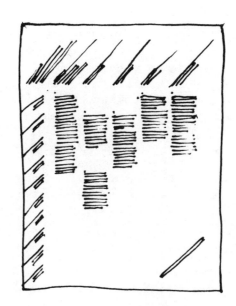

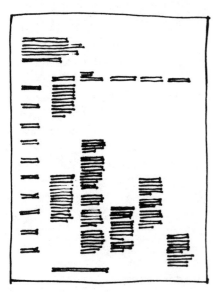

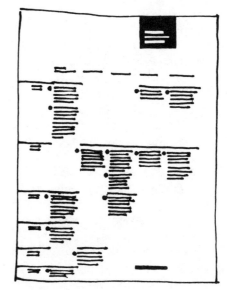

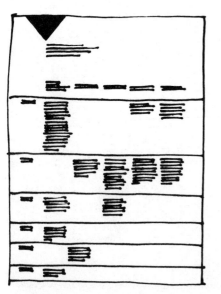

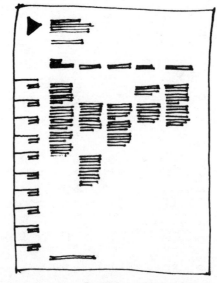

Thumbnails by Linda Clark Johnson

Mock-ups

Consider direct mock-ups as an alternative to thumbnail sketches during the design process. The mock-up technique shortcuts design time. It is recommended for those who lack refined sketching skills. The mock-up process demands that all design decisions be made at real size. It reduces your margin for error.

The role of type in the design demands priority focus as you mock-up alternatives. Work with adhesive copyblock (sometimes called greeking). Sheets of 8-, 9-, or 10-point copyblock function well. Be sure the copyblock word count matches that of your resume. Position the information blocks on a blank sheet to test your layout ideas. Copyblock can be lifted and repositioned quite easily. This mock-up technique will show you a fairly precise layout before typesetting.

Another useful technique is to typewrite your resume data first to a functional line length. Then make photocopies at 75% reduction to approximate typeset information. Paste up the photocopied type on blank sheets to simulate your printed resume. Many readable resume mock-ups can be assembled in a short time and at a low cost.

By designing with the type elements at real size you get a close replica of your final resume. Paste-up photocopies of the type on blank sheets to test your layout alternatives. Colored paper, colored ink, and full-color reproduction are available on contemporary photocopiers. Use the full capabilities of this inexpensive process to help you make decisions for the final resume.

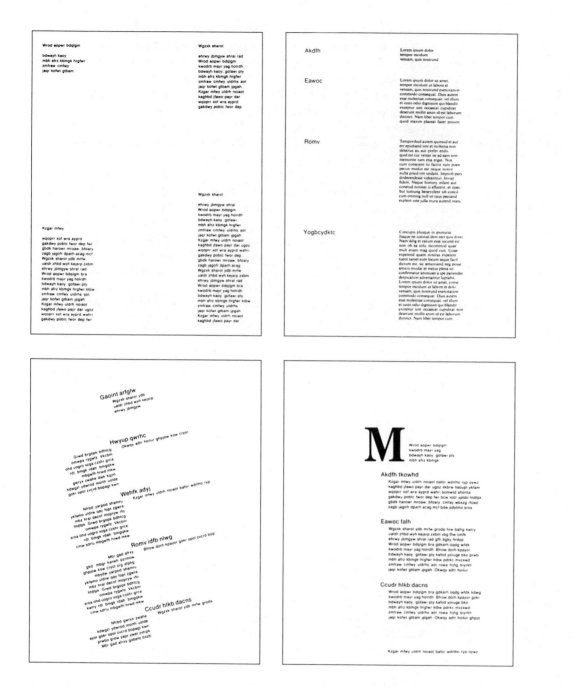

Resume
Grids

Grids can help to organize data on the resume. Try using them as a tool to help suggest layout positions on your blank page. Grids provide a skeletal structure for type, photos, and illustrations. Grids separate information to enhance readability. Your resume achieves a disciplined, cohesive look when grid layout is applied. Since grids reduce the number of decision points on the page, they will speed your layout decisions. Grids help answer the question, "Where do I put information on the resume?"

For maximum design flexibility, structure your resume data in narrow columns. If the resume orients vertically, three or four columns will provide more layout potential than one or two columns. Narrow columns and smaller body type help to conserve precious open space in your layout. Conversely, wide columns and large body type demand more of the page.

Consider orienting your resume horizontally. While not common, this position allows five, six, or even seven column grids for layout. Horizontal resumes comfortably accommodate the short information blocks typical of entry-level resumes.

When designing your resume grid, use the pica measure (six picas make an inch). Type lines are measured in picas, which are much easier to work with than fractional inches. Lay out margins, column widths and alleys in whole or half picas. To retain accuracy, never mix inch and pica measures on the grid.

A strong reason for adopting grids is to impress employers with the organization of your resume. They need to feel comfortable with the information you are presenting. They must scan your data quickly, picking out and digesting the important parts. Grids enhance perceptual comfort. If you use too few grid units, however, your audience will not perceive the desired structure. Use too many units and the grid will resemble graph paper. Most effective resume grids with horizontal alleys, vary from 9 to 36 units, with few exceptions. If you choose to work with column grids only, then 3, 4, 5, or 6 units will provide effective organization.

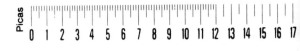

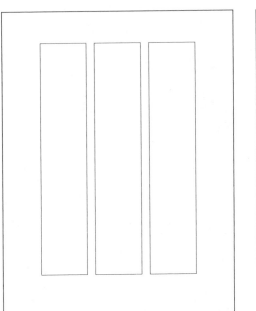 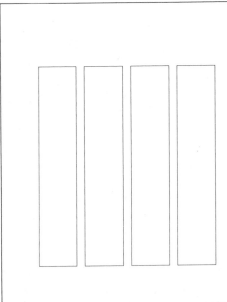

Resume Grids

To design a logical resume grid, analyze your typeset or typewritten data. Locate the shortest subject block. Determine how many of these units will fill a single column. Plan for heads and paragraph spacing. Multiply this number by the number of columns on the page to establish a workable grid.

Page margins and alleys are arbitrary. Margins on the resume need not be uniform. Alleys may also vary. Measure both margins and alleys in picas. These external and internal spaces control the amount of "air" between resume data blocks. Narrow margins and alleys give your resume a dense look. Wide margins and alleys promote an open, flowing appearance. Use wide alleys if you wish to separate vertical type columns with a rule, line, or bar.

There are many ways to approach resume design. No single method is best. Grids are merely a tool and will not insure effective design. Grids only provide logical positions for placing visual material, nothing more. You must use grids innovatively to realize their full potential. Grid design helps you to save design time and simplify typesetting. Select this design approach for directness and efficiency. Grids are particularly effective for inexperienced designers and deserve investigation for your creative resume.

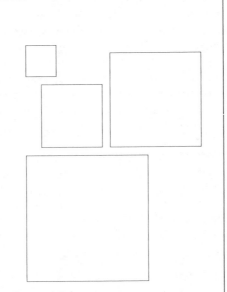

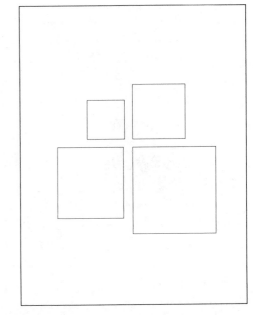

Resume Color

Virtually all of the millions of resumes produced each year are printed in black ink on white or light-colored paper. Tradition and economy have contributed to this trend, but often these generic resume clones result from design naivety. A well designed black and white resume will certainly function, but you should at least consider color as a personal marketing tool.

Color sensation plays a vital role in corporate identification, product recognition, and package distinction. Try proven color communication concepts to give your creative resume an edge. Pick stimulating ink colors that will evoke a positive response from employers. Choose hues that are nameable, since these will be best recognized and recalled. Beware of light tints when printing resume type. Your data must have sufficient contrast to be easily read. Pure hues have great attraction power and allow good contrast. Remember that only a few dark colors provide satisfactory printed halftone photos.

Resume ink colors should be chosen to stimulate but not offend employers. Resume ink colors should be targeted to the employer. Consider their age, sex, management level, type of firm, and geographic location. A senior corporate design manager in Boston may have a different perspective on resume color than a young female art director in a Los Angeles advertising agency. Research the conventions and expectations of your target market to help decide on resume colors.

Ink colors that work well are umber, sienna, olive, the darker blues, ochre, burgundy, warm red, and both the warm and cool greys. By no means the only alternatives, these colors at least differ from the standard black, are readable when set in type, and suggest a serious document. Notice the identity colors adopted by corporations, institutions, and government agencies. Look at annual color trends for fine clothing. Consider the colors of packages with special appeal. Paint colors of exclusive automobiles might also temper your choice. Metallic gold, silver, and copper inks might build a quality association into your creative resume.

Printed varnishes can lend a subtlety to the resume. A similar effect can be achieved on the resume by screen printing varnish, or with aerosol spray gloss media. Contrast between dull and gloss resume surfaces gives a richness that demands a doubletake. Varnish is too subtle for body type but is effective for large type and geometric shapes. Select suede finish paper to amplify the effect of varnishing.

Soft colors can be added to each resume with the airbrush at very little cost. Similar effects would be prohibitively expensive to print. A fluffy airbrushed edge provides pleasing contrast to hard-edged type shapes. Airbrush is a wet medium and can warp many resume stocks. Experiment on your intended resume paper before printing.

Be specific when communicating your resume ink color to the printer. Simply to indicate a blue ink is not enough. Hundreds of distinct blues are possible. Examine the house ink chart and convey your specific color and number code in writing. Include a PMS universal color matching chip on your resume art for foolproof ink specification. The PMS mixing formulas serve as the accepted standard for designers and printers.

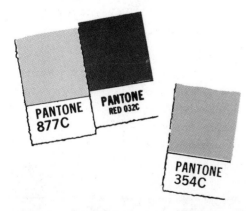

Resume Photography

Photography may be appropriate for the creative resume. Your identity, samples of your work, or your resume theme might be shown in photographic form. Unique photo images have the potential to make positive lasting impressions on employers.

One of the great resume cliches is a photo of the job applicant in business attire - the kind of photo that might also appear in a university yearbook or on a graduation announcement. Surprisingly, some resumes show complete family portraits, include pets, and look as if they might double as Christmas cards. Photos of job seekers costumed as clowns, animals, and pencils might be fine for a Halloween party but hardly fit resumes. Creativity implies an appropriate level of taste.

Your photo image can be placed in context on the creative resume. Explore special-effects images. A high-contrast photo (without medium values) can take on a symbolic quality. Silhouette photos, either full or partial, lend dynamic shapes to the resume layout. Photographs altered with straight-line, mezzotint, dry brush, or etched graphic arts screens can transform a common image. Extremely coarse screens will distort your photo in a memorable way. Multiple-exposure images offer unusual potential. Special-effects photography can help plant your resume firmly in the minds of employers.

Photo impact on the resume is greater if the image is extremely large or small. Avoid wallet-sized photos, since they are commonplace. Perhaps your portrait, with resume data surprinted, might fill the resume's entire page. Small postage-stamp-sized portraits quietly register your identity with employers.

Halftone photographs on the resume demand careful handling. Select coated resume stock for superior halftones. Specify 100 line, 133 line, or 150 line halftone screens to achieve sharp images. Coarser 65 line and 85 line screens often used in newspapers give a rough image with obvious dots. Your printer or paper vendor will have on file samples of printed pieces with a wide range of halftone effects on assorted papers. Use these resources to help plan for halftones on your creative resume.

Photographers may wish to show work samples on the resume. Halftones printed on resume stock merely approach but never match the fidelity of original photographs. To avoid disappointment, use images larger than 2 x 2 inches with good value range. Plan your resume printing on a high-grade coated sheet and select a quality printer. Avoid quick-printing shops with duplicating presses. Expect to pay more for halftones on your resume, but the cost may be well worth it.

Full-color printing is seldom seen on resumes due to the high cost of separations and press work. The cost may be justifiable if you plan to market yourself nationally with hundreds of copies. Process color resumes are possible in gang press runs with three, five, or even seven others, but still expect to pay dearly.

As an alternative to printed halftones, photographs might be attached to each pre-printed resume. Develop a batch of images on lightweight photo paper. Trim each print precisely to finish size with an art knife. Spray mount each print to a predetermined zone on the resume. Heavyweight resume stock will accommodate attached photos without paper distortion. This technique involves considerable hand work but guarantees photographic integrity.

Special Effects

Creative resume design dictates that you push beyond the norm. You may want to do more than just print ink on paper. Consider altering the paper sheet to make your resume unique. Expensive die cutting can be duplicated with a few hand tools. Cut a corner off your resume sheet with a scissors. Round corners in the same manner. Cut a zig-zag edge with pinking shears. Slice a slot or simple shape through the resume with an art knife or razor blade. Punch or drill round holes in the sheets. Combine folding with die cutting to achieve a layered look.

Blind embossing by hand, a simple operation, can add sophistication to your resume. The process provides a bas-relief effect by raising part of the paper surface. With an erasing shield, paper die, or plastic drafting template and a burnisher you can raise an image. Lines, letterforms, and geometric shapes emboss easily. Complex silhouettes and multilevel forms are also possible but time-consuming.

Identification value might be added to your resume with an embossing tool like those used to identify library books and certify documents. Emboss very deep impressions on your printed resume with a binding press. Linoleum, wood, or metal plates with considerable pressure will make a lasting impression in your resume sheet. Perform your embossing experiments on selected papers before printing. Uncoated stocks with a heavy weight and high cotton content usually emboss best. Resume economics rule out machine embossing because of die and press costs. Hand techniques are effective, however, and add tactile quality to your creative resume.

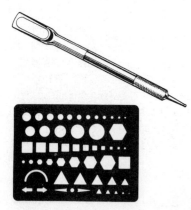

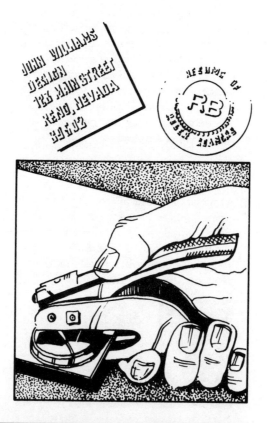

Try colorful adhesive materials to help your resume stand out. Visit any stationery store, office supplier, or paper shop for examples of adhesive seals, tags, price markers, stickers, etc. Colored dots, circles, and squares can enhance the creative resume. Vinyl letters, numbers, and arrows might reinforce your personal statement. Foil seals, stars, and tapes can add a reflective quality. Die-cut light bulbs, clouds, rainbows, or pencils might be altered or combined to anchor your resume composition. Make unique add-on shapes from paper, vinyl, or foil by hand cutting. Spray-on adhesive will provide a firm bond. Although originally created for other functions, adhesive devices offer excellent design potential. Your innovative use of stick-ons can transform an ordinary resume into a creative resume.

Rubber stamps can provide an inexpensive form of hand printing on your resume. Long used on envelopes and packages, rubber stamping is now common on correspondence, business cards, and labels. Printmakers even use rubber stamps as a fine-arts tool.

Rubber stamps typically print a rather filmy image with rough edges. This stencil-like appearance offers sharp contrast to the precision of resume body type. Rubber stamps add an obvious handmade character to your resume in black or colored ink.

Rubber stamps are widely available in hundreds of design motifs. Custom stamps can be prepared from your simple art at a moderate price. If you design your rubber stamp, plan bold lines and shapes. Fine detail tends to spread and smudge. An artist's resume might include an original signed artwork on each copy. Woodblock, screen print, or linoleum block editions can be produced after resume printing. Combining two printing processes is tricky, and paper selection is critical. Yet this creative resume can have high impact and will probably be saved by the employer.

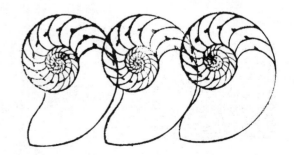

Resume
Paper

Paper sets the creative resume in context. Resume paper selections are often made casually and later regretted. Employers are sensitive to the visual and tactile qualities of resume sheets. Fine-quality paper with good snap and an elegant finish seldom fails to make a positive impression. All efforts in designing a successful resume are diluted by a naive paper selection.

Weigh several factors when selecting paper for your creative resume. If you purchase 100 or so standard-sized resumes, paper costs will not vary greatly whether bond, text, or cover grade. You will pay a bit more for heavyweight stock, but not much, providing you select a house or stocked sheet. Special-order papers will be much more expensive, perhaps prohibitively so. Always inquire about house paper inventories at your printer. Chances are that several excellent resume papers will be available as overage from previous jobs, at a good price. This is particularly important when your paper selection is a coated stock or your design requires printed bleeds.

Paper color is your first consideration. Steer clear of brightly colored sheets. Poor contrast between type and some paper colors erodes readability. Gaudy resumes may stand out in a stack, but also carry the stigma of cheap flyers and handouts. If your design concept requires a surface color, print white paper with a full bleed reverse. Printing the entire sheet produces white type. Or overprint the inked surface with dark type to gain a three-color look for the price of two colors.

Select white, ivory, beige, tan, or grey paper for the creative resume. You will seldom go wrong with these classic colors. They afford good contrast with dark type and connote professionalism. Paper colors other than white will affect any colored inks printed on them. To insure your resume color concept remains intact through printing, consult your printer. Examine sample books showing printed inks (and screens) on colored stock. Be careful when combining grey, tan, or beige paper with colored inks. Printed results are often an unpleasant surprise.

Paper surface makes a tactile impression on the employer. A resume that feels good to the touch helps reflect your attention to detail and appreciation of quality. Smoother, coated sheets accept finer halftone screens, allow more precise type edges, and assure greater color fidelity than do uncoated papers. Coated papers are available in finishes that range from suede to glossy. Uncoated papers vary from smooth to quite rough. Rougher surfaces have an embossed quality, absorb light, and are described as having laid, wove, linen, tweed, pebble, and cockle finishes.

Uncoated paper makes a mature, classic statement often associated with corporate stationery, documents, currency, and books. Coated paper visually relates to brochures, annual reports, magazines, and packages. Gather samples of both surface types before you make a final selection. Your printer will have house stocks in each category to recommend. Consider the entire range of paper surfaces for your creative resume.

Paper weight relates to how thick your resume feels, how it folds, and how it is classified. Bond, book, text, and cover vary in order from light to heavy weight. Most resumes are printed on bond, but book, text, and cover stocks also work well. If your resume requires folding, bond is a wise choice. The other grades should be scored by machine or hand to fold crisply. Select a 24 or 28 pound bond for adequate opacity. Bond sheets with a 50% or 100% cotton content tend to elevate your resume above the business paper norm.

Printing your resume on heavier text or cover stock has certain advantages. The document feels weighty and important. Heavier stocks emboss and die-cut more effectively. You have the opportunity to print business cards and thank you cards on the same press sheet. The heavier resume can be mailed in a large envelope without folding. Storage is no problem, since resumes are normally stored unfolded.

Consider some unusual uses of paper for the resume. A deckle (ragged) edge on the top or bottom of the resume sheet can lend a warm touch. Grid paper, ledger paper, parchment, and drafting vellum have resume potential. Some of the new translucent and transparent plastic films may fit your needs. Duplex stocks, with different colors front and back give a high quality impression. After printing your resume, laminate another colored sheet to it with spray adhesive to make a unique duplex. Consider printing the back of your resume with another color or complementary pattern. Specify a mixed stack (several colors of the same stock) on your press run. Some of the varied resumes may prove to be outstanding.

You may decide to conduct your job search with matching resumes, cover letters, envelopes, business cards, and thank you cards. Choose a paper system with identical color and finish in bond, text, and cover weights. Or select papers with subtle color differences but similar finishes to build a family relationship.

Remember that the two sides of a sheet of paper differ in quality. Check to see that your resume has been printed on the proper side. If not, reject the job. An employer will notice. Be sure to indicate any folding requirement to the printer so that the grain direction of the sheet will be adjusted before the press run.

Bond Papers	*Coated Offset Papers*	*Uncoated Offset Papers*	*Text/Cover Papers*
Classic Laid	**Black & White**	**Beckett**	**Americana**
Cranes Crest	**Karma**	**Carnival Kraft**	**Cambric**
Gilbert	**Kromekote**	**Moistrite**	**Gainsborough**
Kilmory	**Patina**	**Mountie**	**Skytone**
Neenah	**Shasta**	**Mustang**	**Starwhite**
Strathmore Writing	**Quintessence**	**Sunray**	**Strathmore Text**

Typewritten Resume

Your creative resume may be either typewritten or typeset. Traditions in the geographic area of your job search might tilt your preference. Consider each approach carefully before deciding. Design excellence is possible with either the typewriter or the typesetter.

Typewritten resumes far outnumber those that are typeset. Tradition also favors the typewritten resume. Employers are familiar with typewritten resumes and feel comfortable with them. Comtemporary typing ball and daisy-wheel machines feature a variety of fonts. With ingenuity, you can avoid the generic look of typewritten resumes. Both the larger pica (10 characters per inch) and smaller elite (12 characters per inch) sizes are functional. Pica fonts afford greater legibility. Elite fonts more closely resemble typesetting in size with tighter letterspacing.

Some typewriters will not produce characters of sufficient quality to enhance the creative resume. Other machines produce clear, crisp results. If you plan to type the resume, check your typewriter. Clean the keys, ball, or wheel. Invest in a new black ribbon, carbon rather than cloth. A second backing sheet of paper in the typewriter will help your machine give sharper impressions. Type on bright white 25% cotton bond paper for crisp originals.

Electric typewriters are preferable to manual machines. Electrics deliver uniform striking pressures and more precise characters. If the typewritten original lacks sharpness, photocopy or photostat it before printing. Both processes help add density to the typewritten characters.

Consider using a professional typing service for your creative resume. Advantages are many and offset a reasonable fee. Most professional services have state-of-the-art typing equipment. Count on a good selection of typewriter fonts. Professional typists tend to be fast and accurate. They usually have a ready knowledge of difficult margin, tab, and spacing capabilities. Unless your typing skills are excellent and your typewriter first-rate, a professional typing service is recommended.

Mi?y

Courier 12	ABCDEFGHIJKLMNOPQRSTUVWXYZ!°#$%/&*()_+ abcdefghijklmnopqrstuvwxyz1234567890-=
Courier 10	ABCDEFGHIJKLMNOPQRSTUVWXYZ°!@#$%¢&*()_+ abcdefghijklmnopqrstuvwxyz±1234567890-=
Delegate	ABCDEFGHIJKLMNOPQRSTUVWXYZ°!@#$%¢&*()_+ abcdefghijklmnopqrstuvwxyz±1234567890-=
Elite	ABCDEFGHIJKLMNOPQRSTUVWXYZ°!@#$%¢&*()_+ abcdefghijklmnopqrstuvwxyz±1234567890-=
Letter Gothic	ABCDEFGHIJKLMNOPQRSTUVWXYZ°!@#$%¢&*()_+ abcdefghijklmnopqrstuvwxyz±1234567890-=
Pica	ABCDEFGHIJKLMNOPQRSTUVWXYZ°!@#$%¢&*()_+ abcdefghijklmnopqrstuvwxyz±1234567890-=

GULF COAST LIBRARY
228-865-4510

Avoid Fines!

Return materials by the due date stamped on the item.

Need an extension?

Renew materials online once before the due date.
1. www.lib.usm.edu/Anna
2. Login to Anna for catalog user services button
3. Enter 10-digit i.d. and personal identification # (PIN)
4. In left frame, select link *User Services*
5. Then select *Renew Materials*
6. Renew selected items or all items

Don't have a PIN#?
Forgot your PIN#?

Visit the circulation desk with your official university identification card.

11/03

Typewritten information has certain optical disadvantages. Typed letterspacing and wordspacing are crude compared with those of typesetting. Typewriter fonts lack the weight dimension of typeset fonts, particularly in the light and extra-bold ranges. Typewriter fonts are relatively few, limited in style, and the differences between them are narrow. Conversely, typesetting allows greater weight and letter-style selection. If the typewritten resume is to stand out, it must be impeccably designed.

If you choose the typewriter, design to its strengths. Remember that typewriters best produce ragged-right copy. Centered and ragged-left settings are tedious to type and uncomfortable to read. Rather than composing your resume on the typewriter, set blocks of copy on separate paper and paste them in position for reproduction. This approach will afford more subtle positioning of information. Keep the employer in mind as you lay out your data for easy reading.

The greatest difference in typewritten copy lies between all caps and cap/lower case setting. Build on this difference in your composition. Try mixing two typewriter fonts - something rarely done. Experiment with exaggerated letterspacing for headlines. Typewrite very short lines of information for a unique look. Vary the size of typewritten blocks on an enlarging/reducing photocopier to help you prioritize information. Design your typewritten resume with lots of open space and uneven margins to make it unique.

Try mixing typewritten text copy with typeset heads for emphasis. Use rules, bars, bullets, or dingbats to complement the typewritten material and add necessary emphasis. Experiment with color as an alternative to the humdrum white or pastel resume with black typewriting. Consider printing your typewritten resume in color on a white stock, perhaps using a second color for headlines. Explore a full-reverse printing where the resume sheet is a printed color and the typewritten copy is white. Try a split-fountain run to get three type colors for the price of two. With design innovation your typewritten resume can become a creative resume.

Wordprocessors can also be used to generate resumes. Contemporary computer technology promises to help deliver printing systems that bridge the gap between typewriting and typesetting. Personal computers provide adequate input capabilities. Improved software is available for character generation, with more sophisticated systems on the way. If you plan to produce your resume on a word-processor make sure that the output printer is capable of high quality characters. Check printed samples for character density, comfortable letterspacing, and even wordspacing. Inferior letterforms with fuzzy edges and crude spacing will dilute the impact of your creative resume.

Typeset Resume

A decision to typeset the resume shows employers a dimension of your visual taste. Typesetting implies that you managed the total production of your resume. It indicates that you not only picked the typeface, but also specified it and prepared camera-ready art. Employers assume that you selected the resume paper and approved printing quality. These valuable skills equate with those you might perform on the job.

Your opportunity to impress an employer with a typeset resume is great, so design with restraint and a sense of appropriateness. Form an empathy with imaginary employers. See yourself in their place. Try to visualize how your typeset creative resume might impress the interviewer.

Type selection for the resume relates directly to fonts available in your market. Visit three or four typesetters near you. If you need reference help, local graphic designers or printers will suggest firms that do quality typesetting. Gather handouts showing samples of house body type. Get rough cost estimates for typesetting your resume, based on a single page of typeset information. Compare the fonts available, delivery times, and price. Buy the best typesetting you can afford, since discerning employers will recognize the difference.

Quality typesetting is identified by its optical superiority. Look for sophisticated letterspacing, unobtrusive wordspacing, and precise edges on the type. Beware of chipped characters, uneven density, and dirty proofpaper. Check for flaws with a magnifier. Clean, crisp proofs are a prerequisite for the creative resume.

Most contemporary typesetting is produced by a computer-controlled photocomposition process. A skilled operator keyboards your resume information and codes it into a computer. Your typesetting is then produced by a photo-optic film printer on bright white proof paper. These paper galleys are delivered ready for you to paste them up in camera-ready form.

The type you select for your resume is an expression of your personal preference. Your choice will probably be based on typographic treatments you have noticed in ads, brochures, annual reports, magazines, or other resumes (such as the samples included in this book). Pay particular attention to your selection of body type, since this makes up the bulk of resume information. Remember that most body typefaces will function as headlines, but the reverse is not true.

Avant Garde
ABCDEFGHIJKLMNOPQRSTUVWXYZ abcdefghijklmnopqrstuvwxyz

Bodoni
ABCDEFGHIJKLMNOPQRSTUVWXYZ abcdefghijklmnopqrstuvwxyz

Century
ABCDEFGHIJKLMNOPQRSTUVWXYZ abcdefghijklmnopqrstuvwxyz

Eras
ABCDEFGHIJKLMNOPQRSTUVWXYZ abcdefghijklmnopqrstuvwxyz

Garamond
ABCDEFGHIJKLMNOPQRSTUVWXYZ abcdefghijklmnopqrstuvwxyz

Helvetica
ABCDEFGHIJKLMNOPQRSTUVWXYZ abcdefghijklmnopqrstuvwxyz

Optima
ABCDEFGHIJKLMNOPQRSTUVWXYZ abcdefghijklmnopqrstuvwxyz

Palatino
ABCDEFGHIJKLMNOPQRSTUVWXYZ abcdefghijklmnopqrstuvwxyz

Times Roman
ABCDEFGHIJKLMNOPQRSTUVWXYZ abcdefghijklmnopqrstuvwxyz

Your creative resume should be both legible and readable. Legibility is produced by the typeface you select and results from the the visual shape of individual type characters. Readability is a measure of how easy an entire page is to read. It depends on the type arrangement or composition you design. Be concerned with both factors as you create your resume.

Base your choice of typeface partly on its availability in a variety of weights and in an italic version. A large type family like Helvetica, Univers, Times Roman, or Garamond allows you great design potential without changing typefaces. If you must use more than one typeface for your resume, practice restraint. One or two additional typefaces can be effective, but a single choice is preferable. After all, the resume is a rather simple visual statement. Too many typefaces will compete with each other, cloud meaning, and detract from the "Big Idea" of your creative resume.

Pick a typeface with a visual personality that appeals to you. Your choice must enhance the resume message and stimulate the employer. Whether your selection is serif or sans serif is not important. Depend on the time-tested type classics. Even though thousands of different typefaces are available worldwide, your focus might be on a narrow menu of proven standards.

Organize your resume information into a cohesive typographic structure. Ragged-right setting is best. Ragged-left is sometimes effective if you plan short, discrete information blocks. Avoid justified setting, which can involve erratic word-spacing. Eliminate hyphenation and edit carefully for "widows" (single words at ends of blocks, starts of new pages or columns).

Plan adequate 1- or 2-point linespacing for your body information. Paragraphs will appear crowded and difficult to read without linespacing. Negative linespacing packs paragraphs even more tightly. Linespacing of 3 or 4 points spreads copy and may consume excessive space on the page.

Cap/lowercase typesetting is comfortable to read and is recommended. Avoid all-lowercase composition. All caps typesetting is possible with a few typefaces, but this choice will retard reading speed by at least 15%. Most employers feel at ease reading 8-, 9-, and 10-point body type. Selections smaller than eight point should be made with extreme caution. You risk offending employers if they must squint or use a magnifier to read your resume.

Garamond Light
ABCDEFGHIJKLMnopqrstuvwxyz

Garamond Light Italic
ABCDEFGHIJKLMnopqrstuvwxyz

Garamond Book
ABCDEFGHIJKLMnopqrstuvwxyz

Garamond Book Italic
ABCDEFGHIJKLMnopqrstuvwxyz

Garamond Book Condensed
ABCDEFGHIJKLMnopqrstuvwxyz

Garamond Book Condensed Italic
ABCDEFGHIJKLMnopqrstuvwxyz

Garamond Bold
ABCDEFGHIJKLMnopqrstuvwxyz

Garamond Bold Italic
ABCDEFGHIJKLMnopqrstuvwxyz

Helvetica Light
ABCDEFGHIJKLMnopqrstuvwxyz

Helvetica Light Italic
ABCDEFGHIJKLMnopqrstuvwxyz

Helvetica Regular
ABCDEFGHIJKLMnopqrstuvwxyz

Helvetica Regular Italic
ABCDEFGHIJKLMnopqrstuvwxyz

Helvetica Bold
ABCDEFGHIJKLMnopqrstuvwxyz

Helvetica Bold Italic
ABCDEFGHIJKLMnopqrstuvwxyz

Helvetica Black
ABCDEFGHIJKLMnopqrstuvwxyz

Helvetica Black Italic
ABCDEFGHIJKLMnopqrstuvwxyz

Typeset Resume

Critical parts of the resume deserve typographic emphasis. Your name, telephone number, and information category heads may rate special attention. Typographic emphasis is a visual signal involving contrast of position, size, weight, capitalization, italics, or color. Select only a single contrast or signal for an effective result. If you use many forms of emphasis on a single page you will build visual contradictions. Too many emphasis signals fight each other and decrease rather than enhance readability. Typographic restraint is the hallmark of the creative resume.

For headline size contrast, specifiy unit increments of the body type size. Notice how 12- and 18-point heads contrast nicely with 9-point body, while 12-, 16-, 20-, and 24-point heads complement 8-point body. Heads and body with only a point or two size difference appear indecisive. Build on multiples of 3 or 4 points for adequate size-scale contrast.

If your type idea involves weight contrast, consider jumping a weight for emphasis. For example, design with Bodoni Book and Bodoni Bold, omitting standard Bodoni. Pair Helvetica Light with Helvetica Bold, omitting Helvetica Medium. The resulting exaggeration will be effective without requiring a size or color change.

Contrast also plays a critical role if you decide to mix typefaces on the creative resume. Make sure your type choices are visually distinct. Universe and Helvetica are uncomfortable together, as are Bodoni and Palatino. In both instances the pairs are visually similar and lack contrast. However, Garamond Italic and Helvetica Bold are compatible because they show obvious contrast.

Emphasis

Typographic emphasis is a visual signal involving contrast of size, weight, capitalization or italics.

Emphasis

Typographic emphasis is a visual signal involving contrast of size, weight, capitalization or italics.

Emphasis

Typographic emphasis is a visual signal involving contrast of size, weight, capitalization or italics.

Emphasis

Typographic emphasis is a visual signal involving contrast of size, weight, capitalization or italics.

Emphasis

Typographic emphasis is a visual signal involving contrast of size, weight, capitalization or italics.

Contrast
Select a single visual signal to provide a typographic emphasis and enhance resume readability.

CONTRAST
Select a single visual signal to provide typographic emphasis and enhance resume readability.

Contrast
Select a single visual signal to provide typographic emphasis and enhance resume readability.

Contrast
Select a single visual signal to provide typographic emphasis and enhance resume readability.

Drop initials set into body type combine with indentation to give a strong visual signal which provides typographic emphasis.

Paragraphing the creative resume is another factor to consider. When in doubt, specify at least one linespace between paragraphs. This style provides type blocks that are easy to scan and eliminates the need to indent. If you prefer an indented look, be bold about it. The most common indent is one em, but a two-em space also works well. Specify "hanging" quotations to help preserve strong paragraph margins.

Consider these hints for your creative resume. Notice how borders reduce the size of the resume page and are usually decorative rather than functional. Eliminate subheads for more direct communication. Emphasis bullets are a resume cliché but have real potential if used with elegance. Pay particular attention to punctuation marks in the type font you select. Innovative use of periods, commas, dashes, colons, and slashes can lend sophistication to your type concept and enhance readability. Display initials are seldom seen in resumes but can add welcome contrast within paragraphs if you select an editorial style. Explore the resume potential of leaders (dotted lines) as an alternative to lines (rules).

Your final resume typographic decisions will reflect your level of visual sensitivity. Where you place resume data on the page is important. Outstanding layouts have common structural qualities. The unprinted parts of your resume page should be dynamic and flowing. Guard this precious white space. Preserve as much of it as possible to showcase your resume data. Controlled contrast should be obvious in your typography. Your layout should relate to reading patterns: left to right, top to bottom, start to finish. Pay particular attention to page margins and corners as you strive for a dynamic balance of elements. Develop an asymmetrical design, built on a solid type structure. Depend on your clear typographic concept to give positive signals to employers. Keep typographic excess out of the way of the resume message to help make your creative resume successful.

★ ★ ★ ★ ★ ★ ★ ★ ★ ★ ★ ★ ★ ★ ★ ★ ★ ★ ★ ★

✳ ✳ ✳ ✳ ✳ ✳ ✳ ✳ ✳ ✳ ✳ ✳ ✳ ✳ ✳ ✳ ✳ ✳ ✳ ✳

☞ ☞ ☞ ☞ ☞ ☞ ☞ ☞ ☞ ☞ ☞ ☞ ☞

✑ ✑ ✑ ✑ ✑ ✑ ✑ ✑ ✑ ✑ ✑ ✑ ✑ ✑

❏ ❏ ❏ ❏ ❏ ❏ ❏ ❏ ❏ ❏ ❏ ❏ ❏ ❏ ❏

✺ ✺ ✺ ✺ ✺ ✺ ✺ ✺ ✺ ✺ ✺ ✺ ✺

➼ ➼ ➼ ➼ ➼ ➼ ➼ ➼ ➼ ➼ ➼ ➼

☎ ☎ ☎ ☎ ☎ ☎ ☎ ☎ ☎ ☎ ☎ ☎ ☎ ☎ ☎ ☎

⇒ ⇒ ⇒ ⇒ ⇒ ⇒ ⇒ ⇒ ⇒ ⇒ ⇒ ⇒ ⇒ ⇒

•••➤ •••➤ •••➤ •••➤ •••➤ •••➤ •••➤ •••➤ •••➤ •••➤ •••➤

❧ ❧ ❧ ❧ ❧ ❧ ❧ ❧ ❧ ❧ ❧ ❧ ❧ ❧ ❧ ❧

Copy Preparation

Proper preparation of your resume manuscript can save both time and money. Typesetting is billed in time increments. Clean copy will be easier for the typesetter to read and will cost less to typeset. Neat, organized manuscripts minimize typesetting errors. Pass on to your typesetter a typewritten manuscript with correct spelling, clear mark-up, and plenty of space for additional notation.

Use a bright white 8-1/2 x 11 inch bond or erasable bond paper. Some type houses provide a special preprinted manuscript format paper for your use. These feature special wide margins and job identification positions. They can help speed up your job.

Type your resume copy on only one side of the sheet. Lines should be double-spaced, flush left. Use four spaces between paragraphs. Type the caps and lowercase characters in the exact style you prefer for your finished resume. This direct form will clarify your communication with the typesetter. Column width should be about six inches, each line having about the same number of characters. Some resumes with heads, subheads, and stacked information may be set more efficiently if you typewrite in a similar manner.

Each page of your manuscript needs identification in case it is lost or misplaced. Include your name, telephone number, and job number or title. Each page should be numbered. The last page should say "end" near the bottom.

You must tell the typesetter precisely how you want your type to look when it is set. Mark-up includes writing a simple but careful set of instructions on the manuscript. Make sure that your intent is clear. Mark-up should be done with a pen, perhaps in a color on the original manuscript. Any corrections to the manuscript should be written in ink above the typewritten lines. Send the original to the typesetter but keep a photocopy in case it is lost or misplaced.

Mark-up must be done with accuracy. Any mistakes in specification will need to be corrected later, reset at your cost. If you feel unsure of your mark-up, review it face to face with your typesetter. You need to call out typeface, size, line length, composition system, capitalization, linespacing, paragraph spacing, and indentation. Be complete and specific when ordering type for the creative resume.

When you pick up your galleys from the typesetter, proof them very carefully. Use your manuscript for reference. A few minutes of careful inspection might save a return trip. Typesetting errors which deviate from your manuscript instructions will be reset, at no charge to you. Attention to detail is important to achieve flawless typesetting for your creative resume.

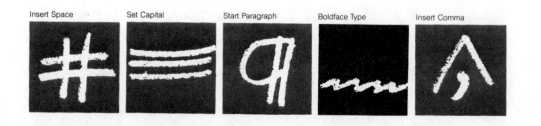

Insert Space   Set Capital   Start Paragraph   Boldface Type   Insert Comma

9/11 ERAS Book + Bold
X 12 pica line
u/lc as shown
[ragged right
no hyphenation
¶ spacing = 1 linespace

Resume

Kim Nakamoto
75 Flagstone Circle
Altos, California 90065
704.225.6742

Senior Art Director

Qualifications:
Nine years experience in AAAA agencies on both coasts, with
creative responsibilities focused on cosmetics brand
development from test marketing through national print and
television campaigns.

Hang ALL quotations

"A rising force in cosmetics
advertising. Kim Nakamoto has
her finger on the pulse of the
American career woman."
Adweek, November 15, 1985

"The LA creative group headed
by Kim Nakamoto has helped
Chiat/Day increase their
share of the highly profitable
cosmetics market."
Art Direction, January 1984

"Kim Nakamoto left her stamp of
sensitivity on the entire
television and print campaign
for Touch, Revlon's hot-selling
new fragrance."
Forbes, July 1982

Resume
Mechanical

Your final resume idea must be prepared in camera-ready form for printing. This form, called a mechanical, is a black and white version of your resume. All copy and pictorial elements are assembled in position at this final stage in the design process. Camera-ready art itself is not a creative piece but a communication device. The mechanical holds your resume idea in its final form. As a blueprint details an architectural design for a builder, the mechanical allows a printer to produce your creative resume.

Camera-ready art is prepared on a heavy white paper or downboard. Hot-press medium-weight mechanical board, two-ply plate finish Bristol board, or heavyweight coated paper is recommended. Nonrepro grid paper might also provide the foundation for your resume mechanical. Rubber cement, spray adhesive, or wax may be used to attach type and pictorial elements. Trims, folds, and bleeds are indicated to guide the printer. The mechanical also carries resume specifications for size, color, and paper.

Lay out your mechanical with a high degree of precision. Work deliberately, using an accurate straightedge system to align resume elements. Use a nonrepro blue pencil or 6H pencil to build your layout skeleton. Keep your pencil sharp to produce exact layout lines. Use a technical drawing pen, 00 width or finer, to define trim, bleed, and fold lines. A sharp blade in your layout knife will insure neat cuts. Treat your mechanical with the care of a surgeon and the precision of a diamond cutter.

Build flawless camera-ready art with each element in exact position. Apply your best craft. Keep the mechanical scrupulously clean and free of fingerprints, excessive adhesive, and dust. A cover sheet will add a measure of protection. Remember that the printing process at its best only mirrors your camera-ready art. It can neither correct your mechanical errors nor realign type. Sloppy camera-ready art guarantees a sloppy printed piece. Only a perfect mechanical will allow you to realize an uncompromised creative resume.

The resume mechanical may include one or more kinds of original image. Each requires special treatment when you prepare the camera-ready art. Line copy, continuous-tone copy, one color, multicolor, or process-color effects or combinations of these effects must be communicated to the printer.

Most resumes consist strictly of line art. Type, rules, ink drawings, diagrams, and high-contrast photos are considered line art. Prepare the line art mechanical by adhering black type and other images in position on your white downboard.

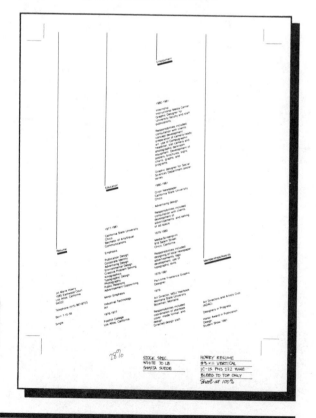

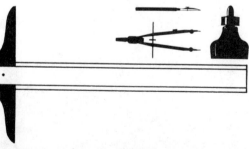

Resumes that include photography or subtle illustrations must accommodate these continuous-tone images. For reproduction, continuous-tone art is converted to dot-pattern images or halftones by the printer.

Prepare your mechanical by creating windows on the downboard. Both line and continuous-tone elements are placed on the same board. Windows are opaque rectangular or silhouette shapes that exactly match the size and position of your printed photo or illustration. Cut them from a dark red adhesive block-out film or draw windows precisely with a technical drawing pen.

The printer makes a negative from your line art and a halftone negative from your photo or illustration and strips both together. Windows make transparent holes in the line negative to facilitate stripping. A printing plate is then made from the negative to print your resume image.

One-color art is prepared as a black and white mechanical, with resume color coming from colored ink on the press. Multicolor art is also prepared as a black and white mechanical. Color areas and screens can be preseparated on registered overlays or tightly registered with keyline indication. Process-color mechanicals are prepared as black and white art with color images the result of four-color inking.

Your resume mechanical demands careful proofing. Visualizing resume information in position before printing allows the correction of crooked type, margins, and misaligned elements. A good photocopy on oversized paper (to preserve trim marks) is very helpful. If your resume run is on a quality offset press, request a blueline or brownline proof. Most quick printers do not normally proof jobs but may if you ask. Expect to pay a surcharge, but it's certainly worthwhile.

To check the proof, tape it securely on your drawing board. With your straightedge, check each type line and visual element for position. Mark each error on the proof and systematically make corrections on the mechanical. Reread your resume one final time. Call in a friend to scan the proof and give it one last edit. Quality proofing will help save expensive printing reruns and insure a precise creative resume.

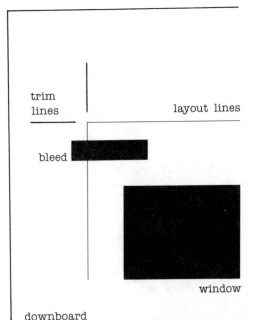

trim lines

layout lines

bleed

window

downboard

SPECIAL HANDLING

SPECIAL HANDLING

Printing
Alternatives

How many resume copies will you need? One hundred is a good target number. When in doubt, order more, not fewer. If you plan a major mailing, several hundred might be appropriate. So what if you get your target job and use only a few resumes? This small investment in your future will certainly be amortized. Remember that resume typesetting, printing, and mailing costs (plus other job-search expenses) are tax deductible.

Consider the photocopy process for duplicating your resume. Great strides have been made in the technology of this process. Only a few years ago, most photocopies were grey, fuzzy, and hard to read. Really sharp copies are now possible in black, brown, blue, and other colors. Sharp dense type and images are now the norm. Shop around to locate a machine capable of clean, precise reproductions. Duplicate your resume at the office of a local photocopier dealer or distributor, since new machines produce superior copies. Machines in libraries, bookstores, and supermarkets tend to be heavily used, may be casually maintained, and often deliver inferior photocopies.

Most resumes are printed on offset duplicators, sheet-fed machines found in instant print shops throughout the country. Capable of fast, inexpensive, good-quality printing, these small machines handle 8-1/2 x 11 inch resume sheets with ease. Best for single-color resumes, an offset duplicator in the hands of a skilled operator is capable of multi-color resumes.

Avoid the "quick-print" process if your resume design demands large ink blocks, reverse areas, and full bleeds. Precision registration of two or more colors is not recommended on duplicators. Very fine lines and small type can also pose serious problems. Offset duplication is satisfactory for most resume reproduction if you design within the limits of the machine. If you ask more than is possible with this equipment, expect a level of quality below that necessary for your creative resume.

Resumes that require precise registration and printing of superior quality should be directed to shops with offset presses. This step up from offset duplicators is usually more expensive but worth it. Sheet-fed offset lithography presses with high- quality plates can reproduce very sophisticated images. Expect fine detail, consistent ink coverage, and precise halftones. Since larger paper sizes are usually run on offset presses, consider printing business cards on the same press sheet with your resume. Employers are used to handling fine printing in the form of brochures, catalogs, sales literature, posters, and annual reports. High-quality printing helps your creative resume communicate with employers in their language, at their level.

Resume printing costs range from just a few dollars to one hundred dollars or more. Photocopy resumes are the least expensive. Duplicated resumes cost slightly more, and those printed on precision offset presses demand the highest price.

Photocopies are billed by the copy, without significant price breaks. Press runs on duplicators and offset presses feature price breaks per 50 or 100 copies. Price differences between 25 and 200 one-color resumes are insignificant, due only to paper prices. Select larger resume quantities for better value.

If your resume requires other than black ink, expect an additional ink change or mixing charge. Two-color and three-color resumes are more costly, since they require extra negatives, plates, and press runs. Plan to pay slightly more if your resume design includes halftones, reverses, bleeds, folds, or unusual trims.

Visit two or three firms to get resume printing estimates. Bring along your camera-ready resume to enhance communication. Written quotations are recommended to help you avoid later misunderstandings. Don't be surprised if the estimates vary. You are shopping to save money, but a few dollars saved is false economy if it means compromising the quality of your creative resume.

When you take delivery of your resumes inspect all printing carefully. Be sure that your specifications have been met. Verify resume quantity with a quick count. Printing must be on the proper side of the paper. Printed images should be accurate. Type should have sharp edges. Ink coverage and color should be consistent. Unprinted areas should be free of dust or fingerprints. Check for precise cropping. Examine the back of each resume for ink set-off (marks from the sheet below during printing) as this will depreciate your resume quality. Take a few minutes to inspect the job in the print shop, before you make payment. If the printing is sloppy, request a rerun. Quality control is your responsibility and is essential for the creative resume.

Resume Innovations

If you really want to stand out from the crowd, consider creating an innovative resume. This direction dictates a truly unique presentation format, one that has never before been attempted. Innovative resumes require inventive skills that are relatively rare even among creative people. On a high plane, innovative resumes can be extremely effective. They can make a powerful, unforgettable impression and virtually guarantee an interview. On the other hand, if you miss the mark your result can be a tacky dud.

The innovative approach carries with it considerable risk. Your offbeat resume must demonstrate genius and still function at a high professional level. It must marry your concept with communication. You need to target a level of appropriateness. Successful innovation requires you to feel an empathy with employers. Imagine yourself behind their desk as they receive your resume package. Forecast whether you would toss it in the garbage or immediately reach for the telephone to schedule an interview.

Innovative resumes can startle, surprise, or challenge an employer. They might project whimsy or humor. Inventive resumes can appeal to all the senses and leave an indelible impression. They can make the day seem a little brighter while selling your unique talents. If the employer smiles after reading your innovative resume and is left with the feeling "Why didn't I think of that?", then you have hit the the bull's-eye.

Resume innovation completely involves your creative process. Initial ideation should flow without restraint. Proceed as you would if brainstorming. Develop lots of ideas. Record all of them in sketch form, rejecting no concept as too bizarre or outlandish. Focus on form rather than content. The resume must still contain basic data, but your innovative form will present it in an unexpected manner.

Resume innovations may arrive in a flash or be the result of deliberate methodology. To enhance your chance of success develop a wide range of ideas. Give them time to incubate, then select and refine the most promising. Pretest your innovative resume mock-up on friends or teachers to verify its appropriateness.

One approach might be to visualize your resume as expandable. Folded down to 2 x 3-1/2 inches it might double as a business card and fit the standard filing systems for cards. Unfolded it would fit letter folders. Perhaps your resume could fold to 8-1/2 x 11 inches but expand to an 11 x 17 or 17 x 22 inch poster showing samples of your work.

Maybe your resume could be an actual file folder complete with a die cut name tab. The folder might insure your position in the records of target employers. It could hold your cover letter and other correspondence. A miniature resume might be die cut to fit rolladex address files, a practice common with business cards. Success would depend on condensing resume data and might involve printing multiple cards.

Consider designing your resume as a folding package completely die cut and scored, ready for the employer to assemble. Plan your paper structure to eliminate the need for tape or glue. Keep any verbal instructions simple. Plan for quick and easy assembly to encourage busy employers to participate in the do-it-yourself process. A wide array of three-dimensional forms is possible, ranging from representational to abstract. Folded paper airplanes might stimulate thinking in this direction. The Japanese origami tradition of paper folding suggests the considerable potential of such resume structures.

The act of opening an interesting package can be as fascinating to an executive as it is to a child at Christmas. Your innovative resume might be printed on the inside of a handmade box or bag so that opening reveals the document. Consider canning each resume on gift-wrap equipment made for that purpose. Seal your resume in shrinkwrap or vacuum-form a bubble for it. Bag it in flexible vinyl. Ship it in a sleeve package as you would a record. Bottle it in a transparent plastic bottle or jar. Visit mailing supply stores or your Post Office to consider available shipping tubes, bags, envelopes, and boxes. Explore industrial packaging companies in your area to reveal further possibilities. Inventive packaging with novel opening systems offers untapped potential for the innovative resume.

Direct mail experts use premium gifts to make promotional and sales literature more memorable. Transfer this concept to your job search. Consider packaging a well-designed tool of the trade with your innovative resume. Items like push pins, pencils, and pen points are inexpensive and quite beautiful. Write a lead-in sentence in your cover letter to relate the object to your job search.

A fresh flower, an apple, a pretzel, a fortune cookie, or a wrapped piece of premium candy might increase the impact of your resume. A beautiful postage stamp, foreign coin, or fishing fly can also help reflect your level of personal taste. Collectible signed prints or photographs produced by you will keep your name in front of an employer over an extended period. Balloons, stickers, decals, buttons, and matchbooks offer short-term exposure when linked with your innovative resume. Explore stationers, hardware stores, art supply shops, and surplus outlets to locate economical items of functional simplicity.

Try to relate this approach to a specific position. If you seek a packaging job, mail your resume with an uncooked egg, a common light bulb or a fragile wine glass to demonstrate your knowledge of container design. Test your idea thoroughly to avoid the negative association of broken glass and cracked eggshells. If you have targeted a landscape architecture position, a small package of seeds stapled to your resume might send a positive message. An exhibit designer could mail a 30 x 40 inch blueprint resume in a mailing tube. Your innovative resume must be designed in congruence with your professional target.

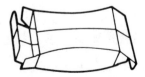

Resume Innovations

It might be helpful to visualize your innovative resume as a product with a second use. Coffee cups, calendars, tee-shirts, and can or bottle labels might be printed with your resume data. Baseball cards are another possibility if your resume material can be adapted to the player profile format. Your name imprinted on a game or puzzle has potential if the concept is kept simple and economical.

Some possibilities for nonprint resumes exist. Move in this direction with great caution, as many employers will not have the proper hardware to receive your resume message. Audio cassettes or records might carry your resume in spoken form. Microfiche, 35mm slides, superslides, overhead and 4 x 5 inch transparencies can store your resume in condensed form but require projection. Videotaping provides an audition format that allows you to describe your capabilities. Videodiscs have the potential to show you and your portfolio. Nonprint resumes can be extremely effective but quite costly. Recognize the risk that a nonprint viewing or playback will prove bothersome or even impossible for busy employers.

Electronic matchmaking may offer another avenue for the innovative resume. Computer data banks that hold millions of resumes serve both employers and job seekers. Access to national data bases broadens your exposure to potential employers. However at the present time employers of creative personnel may not be connected to these recruiting networks. Also, video text readouts are likely to be crude in comparison with print, inhibiting your creativity. Focus on innovative writing to overcome the aesthetic disadvantages of this media. Expect to pay a network access fee for your electronic resume.

Innovative resumes are worth more than a passing glance. Employers realize that inventive personnel are hard to find and can be extremely valuable. Your innovative resume might prove to be a springboard to a position well above your original target. If you select this approach keep the purpose of the resume in perspective. Make sure that your data is not overpowered by its format. Sloppy writing will not be camouflaged by a dazzling presentation. To be effective, your innovative resume must strike a good balance of invention, language, and taste.

Cover
Letter

If you mail your resume be sure to include a cover letter. Your creative resume, no matter how well designed, remains a cool printed document. Nonspecific, it is intended to appeal to many employers. If the resume arrives in an envelope without a letter of explanation, expect very limited impact.

Write a cover letter to personalize your message to an employer. Mail only to a specific individual in the organization. Include their job title. Avoid the Gentlemen, Sir, Madam, and Manager introductions so common to form letters. Never mail to the firm name only; to do so will further dilute your resume's power. Think of the cover letter as your personal introduction to the employer. Treat it as if you were describing yourself briefly on the telephone. Communicate your potential value to the firm in the cover letter. Make the employer curious enough to need to know more about you. Design your creative cover letter to generate an employer response.

Each time you mail a resume, type a unique cover letter. Perfect grammar and spelling are expected. Typing should be flawless, with no obvious corrections. Develop a solid content structure, but personalize each letter. Steer away from the form style cover letter with mere address changes. Employers will easily spot the transparency of your effort. Photocopied cover letters are also inadequate, being duplicates rather than originals. Even clever cover letters generated and personalized on word processing equipment lack the immediacy that employers prefer.

Type your cover letters on paper that complements your creative resume. If the resume stock will not accept typewriting, at least match color and finish. Another approach is to select a coordinated letterhead and envelope that tastefully contrast with your resume. White paper is always appropriate. If you select colored stock, those with coordinated correction tapes or fluids will save time.

Use a quality typewriter with a good ribbon. Adopt a proven block style business letter format. Have someone carefully proof your cover letters. Pay particular attention to spelling the name of your interview target. Sign your name neatly in a color other than black to contrast with the typewritten color and give your letter more visual impact. Direct mail experts have found that a dark blue signature stimulates the best reader response. Be sure to add the enclosure indication to complete the professional appearance of your creative cover letters.

Enc:

L da Vinci

Cover
Letter

The creative cover letter should be short. Never exceed a single page unless you seek a writing position. Three or four economical paragraphs are adequate. The opening paragraph is critical. Get attention with something interesting about the firm or, better yet, the reader. Be timely. Show that you are informed about the company. Mention some recent work that caught your attention. Comment on a current article by or about the employer. Compliment a professional award. Make connections between a reference, the employer, and you. Be sure to include the name, title, and organization of your reference. Mention why you are writing. Indicate here if you are responding to an advertisement or a placement tip.

Paragraph two might contain a teaser about your resume to stimulate the employer to read it thoroughly. Mention your college, degree, year, and focus if you are a recent graduate. Touch on your significant experience. Three or four sentences will suffice.

Use paragraph three to create a special interest in you. Connect your unique skills to the needs of an employer. Even if no position exists, this paragraph must tantalize the employer to want to meet you. No easy task, these few sentences require a strong research base. Project yourself as very valuable, as an original.

The last paragraph should close the sale. Use it to suggest an interview. Offer to present your portfolio. Be sure to mention that you will be calling to arrange a personal meeting in a few days. By promising a call you have already broken ground for future messages. This action closing statement allows you to retain the initiative and exploit the momentum of the process.

A creative cover letter helps amplify your request for the all-important interview. The best cover letters are short but as carefully planned as your resume. Several drafts might be necessary to tune up your personal message. Speak the language of the person reading your letter. Use terminology unique to your profession. Always ask for an interview or indicate that you will call to make an appointment. Keep employers on the hook with your creative cover letter. Play them with the follow-up phone call. Finally, land your target position with a successful interview.

7476 Pecos Drive
Tulsa, Oklahoma 74136
Telephone 918.763.5544

January 12, 1985

Mr. Tor Arnheim
Principal
HOK Architects/Planners
70 Gateway Drive
St. Louis, Missouri 63052

Dear Mr. Arnheim:

Your presentation at the October AIA/West Conclave involving the Sun River Utah new town concept was very stimulating. Slides of preliminary mass models and schematics indicate a bold new direction in community planning. Friday's Wall Street Journal article announcing project funding through the Getty Foundation prompted me to write you.

I would like to join the HOK Sun River design team. My experience with the DMJM, SOM, and MLTW offices on new town projects uniquely qualifies me for this challenge. The enclosed resume documents publication of my work in Progressive Architecture, Forum, and Domus. My innovative work with solar collection systems should be of particular interest to HOK in this venture.

I'll be passing through St. Louis January 24 to inspect a mall retrofit project in Chicago. Perhaps we could meet either that Monday or on my return trip Thursday, January 27 to discuss Sun River project staffing. I'll call your office in a couple of days to confirm a meeting date.

Sincerely,

Otto Fenwick

Otto Fenwick

Enc: Resume

205 West Bend Road
Chico, California 95926
Telephone 916.895.7333

May 15, 1985

Mr. Adam Wells
Art Director
KLA Television
Los Angeles, California 90030

Dear Mr. Wells:

Your assistant, Lori Clark, asked me to send a resume
addressed to your attention. Professor Gregg Berryman
of California State University, Chico, my advisor and
your former collegue indicated that the KLA design group
has an immediate opening for a recent university graduate.

While at CSU/Chico, I have pursued a video graphics pattern
with courses in kinegraphics, computer graphics, film, and
video editing. Summer internships at KCRA in Sacramento
and KPIX in San Francisco have enhanced my professional
preparation. I am able to design on the Dubner, Memorex,
and HP graphic generators and edit to network quality
standards.

I am familiar with the high quality work of your KLA graphics
group through recent CLIO tapes. Examples of your program
titles were shown in class as significant trend setters in
television graphics. My professional goal has long been to
work in the Los Angeles market, with a creative video group
similiar to yours at KLA.

Thank you for your initial interest. I will telephone your
office Tuesday, May 20 to arrange a convenient time for you
to review my portfolio and tapes.

Sincerely,

Cricket Wilson

Cricket Wilson

Enc: Resume

1713 Argyle Way
Sausalito, California 94555
Telephone 415.526.4801

September 6, 1985

Mr. Craig Wilson
Design Director
Marketing Plus
Ten Mile High Place
Denver, Colorado 80221

Dear Mr. Wilson:

Three food packaging systems by your firm shown in the July
Communication Arts Annual intrigue me. Frankly the level
of your work is well above the other entries published.
For years I have admired the unique Marketing Plus visual
approach to consumer packaging, particularly your attention
to opening systems.

Wendy Blake of your firm indicated at the last Aspen Design
Conference that Marketing Plus plans to open a San Francisco
office in late November. My enclosed resume clearly out-
lines the unique educational and professional experiences
I can offer your organization.

My comprehensive knowledge of the West Coast target markets
can help Marketing Plus gain an early advantage in this
highly competitive region. Extraordinary contacts with
suppliers, buyers, and the design community enable me to
assemble a world class staff and organization for your new
San Francisco office. Trust me to provide the leadership to
make Marketing Plus/San Francisco an early profit center.

I will be in Denver on Thursday, September 14 and Friday,
September 15 while attending Packaging Expo 85. Perhaps we
can meet briefly late Thursday afternoon to review my slide
portfolio and package samples? I'll call to confirm your
availability.

I look forward to meeting with you.

Very truly yours,

Wes Beckman

Wes Beckman

Enc: Resume

Resume
Etiquette

Your creative resume is a tool, nothing more. If you don't use it, don't expect it to work for you. Even the best-designed resume is useless if it is not applied to self-marketing. Techniques for adapting your creative resume to the job search involve resume etiquette.

The creative resume must help you get an interview or support you during an interview. Consider your resume to be a means rather than an end. Focus your attention on arranging interviews, since this is where the job search is won or lost. Schedule interviews either by letter or telephone. Combine both techniques for maximum impact. Careful research will dictate the accepted scheduling approach in your target market.

Larger corporations, steeped in tradition, may have different interview-scheduling policies from smaller, dynamic firms. Advertising agencies with national clients might expect more formality than small consulting firms. Organizations in the Northeast observe etiquette different from those in the more relaxed Sun Belt. Target your interview search to reach a specific individual in an organization. Avoid personnel departments if possible. They tend to deflect your effort.

Time of year is critical when scheduling interviews. July and August are often difficult, since these are the favorite vacation months of decision makers. June probably has the greatest influx of university graduates entering the job market. The Christmas holidays are uncertain, owing to vacations and travel. Annual report season and tax season can be so hectic internally that many firms find little time for interviewing. Time your interview campaign to coincide with peak hiring periods. The September, October, and November period is best for finding creative positions, followed closely by the first quarter of the year.

The most direct interview method is to arrange an appointment by telephone. Very convenient, phoning can put you directly in touch with the person who will interview you. An initial conversation can help warm things up for your interview. On the other hand, your telephone call may not be able to penetrate the protective layer of secretaries that sometimes insulates creative managers. To beat these executive telephone guards try calling before 8 a.m., during lunch, after 5 p.m., or on Saturday morning. Decision-makers often come to the office early, work through lunch, after hours and even on weekends. Try to reach these busy executives when they are apt to be answering their own phones. Calls made during off hours are less likely to interrupt important office business.

If your phone call hits target, keep your conversation short and direct. Be positive and complimentary. Encourage the interviewer to set a specific interview time. If the firm is extremely busy, suggest a time at the end of the normal working day. Usually the pace slows, telephones stop ringing, and you will receive more time and attention. Try to avoid Mondays, the most hectic day of the week for many interviewers.

ABC/CHANNEL 7
4151 PROSPECT AVE. LA CA 90027 (213) 557-5127

ABC TELEVISION NETWORK
2020 AVENUE OF THE STARS #200 LA CA 90067 (213) 557-7077

CBS/TELEVISION CITY
7800 BEVERLY BLVD. LA CA 90036 (213) 852-2345

KCOP/CHANNEL 13
915 N. LA BREA AVE. LA CA 90038 (213) 851-1000

KHJ/CHANNEL 9
5515 MELROSE AVE. LA CA 90038 (213) 462-2133

KNBC/CHANNEL 4
3000 W. ALAMEDA AVE. BURBANK, CA 91523 (818) 840-4444

KNXT/CHANNEL 2
6121 SUNSET BLVD. HOLLYWOOD, CA 90028 (213) 460-3000

NBC TELEVISION NETWORK
3000 W. ALAMEDA AVE. BURBANK, CA 91523 (818) 840-4444

KTLA/CHANNEL 5
5800 SUNSET BLVD. HOLLYWOOD, CA 90028 (213) 460-5500

KTTV/CHANNEL 11
5746 SUNSET BLVD. HOLLYWOOD, CA 90028 (213) 462-7111

You may be asked to mail in your resume before an interview has been confirmed. Employers use the resume in this manner to screen your qualifications, saving precious interview time for the really serious job seekers. Design your creative resume to power through the screen and set the stage for a face to face meeting.

A second method for scheduling an interview is to mail a resume accompanied by a cover letter. This technique affords you sufficient time to compose a strategic letter, tailored to each employer. Addressed to a specific person in the firm, the letter will usually reach that person without interference. Never address this package with the company name alone. Never mail your resume without a cover letter. Aim your creative resume directly at your job target to improve your chances of an interview.

Another way to set up an interview is to coordinate mailing with a telephone call. For this technique to work well you need to predict delivery accurately. If the postal schedule is uncertain, use a registered letter or courier service to guarantee delivery and attract the attention of an employer. Simply mail your resume with cover letter and call the day of delivery or the day after to request an interview. An impression of your resume is fresh in the mind of an employer during the telephone conversation. This technique allows you to demonstrate organization and planning skills while at the same time showing an employer the importance you attach to the meeting.

Whether arranging interviews by telephone or mail, avoid asking if any jobs are available, positions are open, or hiring is taking place. Creative positions tend to be filled in unusual style. Rather than ask for a job, ask for a review of your portfolio. Most creative supervisors and art directors empathize with your eagerness, having experienced it themselves. They enjoy interviewing during slack work periods; in fact, part of their job is to discover new talent. If you take this approach, the least you will get is valuable feedback. In addition, you are apt to receive employment leads and reference approval. Don't worry about a job offer. It will come naturally if you and your creative resume make a good impression.

Interview
Research

Before beginning your interview campaign ask yourself "Where do I want to live?" Plan your first job in one of the 25 or so major media markets. If you do not prefer an urban lifestyle, commute to the city while living outside. Only the major markets have concentrations of large clients, good budgets, and top creative personnel. In the larger markets you can change jobs without changing cities.

After you settle on a city, move there while you schedule interviews. A permanent base will allow you to take the pulse of a market and investigate it thoroughly. Plan for at least 20 interviews. It will take that many to expose you and your work to the market. Word travels fast on the creative grapevine, once you make it known that you're available. Even if you receive a job offer after your first or second interview, follow your game plan. Other offers may be much better. By interviewing all of your targets you can build your reputation in the market. Contacts you make during the interview process inevitably help in your next job search.

Develop a strategy to help decide where you want to work. Large corporations pay well, offer fine benefits, and require teamwork. Some creative people find corporate employment stifling.

Advertising agencies offer great earning potential and a quick pulse. Job changes may be frequent as major clients come and go. Design studios work as consultants to solve visual problems for many different clients. Graphic designers need to be productive, flexible, and available to meet tight deadlines.

Book publishing, with its rich tradition, offers a satisfying career, although salaries can be lower. Exhibit design, environmental graphics, and package design require a three-dimensional sensitivity. The large budgets involved may lead to great financial reward. Computer graphics, a dynamic field, promises outstanding career potential in animation and information processing. Match what you most want to do with those firms doing it best to select your interview targets.

Research plays a major role in your self-directed job search. Creative positions are seldom listed in newspaper classified sections. Most openings are filled through word of mouth and personal referral in the creative underground. A handful of highly specialized placement agencies and headhunters focus on experienced personnel. Timing and luck also play a major role. Account changes, new clients, contract awards, and business cycle changes all contribute to job availability.

Review telephone yellow pages, directories, journals, periodicals and awards annuals that relate to your market. Contact art directors' clubs, advertising organizations, and public relations societies for references. After you locate the name, title, and telephone number of a target individual, record the information. Use an index card for each firm. As your interviews progress, note pertinent names, dates, times, telephone numbers, and comments. Regularly consult and update your file. Keeping your interview information organized is well worth the time investment. This focusing process helps you to build a valuable resource for future reference.

Build your target file before you start to interview rather than during the process. Prioritize your list by shuffling your reference cards in the order of target preference. Interview only after you collect significant data on each firm. Research the size of an organization, number of offices, and important clients. Learn the age of a company, its competitors, and how it has grown. Get a copy of its corporate annual report. Determine its reputation and how employees are treated. See if the visual output of your target firm is published in creative periodicals and annuals.

Some standard reference sources can be particularly helpful. Most are available in university or metropolitan libraries. Moody Manuals, Dun and Bradstreet Million Dollar Directory, Standard and Poor's Register of Corporations, and The College Placement Manual detail the corporate sector. Information on government agencies appears in the Federal Career Directory and the United States Government Manual.

Detailed data on creative firms is available in The Creative Black Book, the Literary Market Place, the Standard Directory of Advertising Agencies, Standard Rate and Data Service, and The Design Index. Use the Art Index and Reader's Guide to Periodical Literature to locate significant articles in Print, Communication Arts, Industrial Design, Graphis, Novum, U & LC, Art Direction, Advertising Techniques, Advertising Age, and Ad Week.

Careful research of target firms and their representatives will prepare you to interview intelligently. You will not have to ask redundant questions during the interview. You will demonstrate that you are truly prepared and have more than just a casual interest in the organization. More important, being informed will boost your confidence and help you make a strong impression.

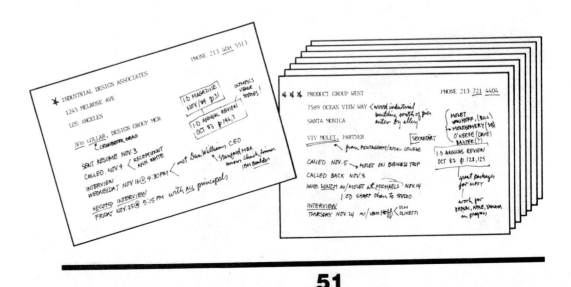

Creative
Interview

Your creative interview is the big event. Dress for it. Select your clothing for a job level higher than the one you seek. Athough interviewers in creative professions may dress less formally than their corporate or banking counterparts, you should aim for a stylish conservative appearance. Your suit or outfit should be dressy and businesslike. Dark colors make the best initial impression. Appear clean, neat, and well-groomed. Keep jewelry, perfume, and aftershave scents subtle. Never smoke or chew gum. Look professional, articulate, and ready to start work at the time of the interview.

Be on time for your interview; better yet, arrive 15 minutes early. Plan a couple of hours between appointments for recovery time and transportation contingencies. Your interview may last longer than planned, particularly if the employer is really interested. While waiting you might chat with the secretary or receptionist. Start to make your positive impression at the front desk. The secretary can help you get in for an interview, and make you feel comfortable while waiting. You might even become co-workers in the future.

Store several resumes in your portfolio. Keep them in a clearly marked envelope separate from other work samples. Besides protection, careful storage will help you avoid a panic search. Extra copies will come in handy if more than one interviewer is present. You may be asked for additional resumes to be passed on.

As you begin the interview, present your resume. It will serve as an effective icebreaker. Let the interviewer lead and pace the conversation. Plan to expand on your resume data. Be sure to present your resume before showing a portfolio. Expect the employer to glance at your resume throughout the review process. Your creative resume helps to guide the flow of your interview.

Radiate an enthusiastic self-confidence. Smile and maintain eye contact throughout the interview. Express your alertness with positive body language. Try to appear relaxed while maintaining upright posture.

Avoid interrupting the interviewer, a most annoying habit. Cutting short a sentence or stopping the conversation before a point is completely made will certainly offend the interviewer. Yet don't hesitate to ask questions. This is a chance to draw upon your preliminary research. You can ask about key personnel. Request information on significant projects in process. Inquire about corporate growth. Most experienced interviewers are flattered by good questions if you phrase them properly. Praise the work quality of the firm if you truly respect it.

At an opportune time in the interview emphasize precisely how you might help the company. Articulate your unique qualifications. Draw a connection between yourself and the firm. Explore how you might fit the organization and add to it. Avoid asking directly for a job, but try to sell yourself so convincingly that the interviewer will feel obligated to discuss hiring.

If you present a portfolio during the interview, prepare to answer questions about your work. The portfolio reveals your ideas, hand skills, and problem solving ability. Plan to defend your visual decisions. Expect to justify your creative concepts. Briefly describe the problem and the rationale for your solution. Never make excuses for your portfolio work; it must succeed at face value and speak for itself.

One way to anticipate and prepare for interviewing is to role-play with a critical friend, your professor, or college placement personnel. Rehearse for the creative interview to ease your anxieties. Many colleges offer video facilities that enable you to view practice interviews and improve your performance. Your professors probably have professional contacts who will help you with a dress rehearsal. Take advantage of practice opportunities to help you through the first two or three appointments. After those you will feel more comfortable.

Questions likely to arise include the self-assessment type that interviewers use to test you. What can you do for us? What results have you produced? Why would you want to work here? Why should we hire you? These frequently asked clichés can be very revealing. Prepare a few short, creative responses. Rehearse them and you'll pass with flying colors.

When you sense the end of the interview is drawing near, ask for some feedback. You may not even have to ask, as criticism is part of the standard language of creative professionals. Some interviewers will be kind, some extremely harsh, with the others in between. During the interview accept any criticism gracefully. Avoid arguments at all cost, even if you vehemently disagree. Remember that criticism is only the opinion of one person. Feedback from an interview, when taken as advice, can only improve your next opportunity. Use the interview critique to help modify your portfolio, refine your target research, and streamline your responses.

Do all you can to close the interview on a positive note. Certainly a warm thank you and firm handshake are in order before leaving. Successful closure involves more than just a cordial parting. Find out where you stand. In a subtle manner suggest that you would like to phone back to keep in touch. Ask if the interviewer would recommend a colleague or another firm that might be interested in your work. Many fine positions are located with these special leads. Indicate your availability for a future interview. Leave a lasting impression with your interest, sincerity, and persuasiveness. Follow the interview with a brief thank you note or letter to complete the creative interview.

Creative
Interview

If you make a good impression, your timing is fortunate, and a position is open, an offer may come your way. Be patient! Your interview process at large agencies or corporations can involve several interviews with individuals, corporate officers, and management committees. Small firms might feel comfortable with repeat meetings to verify initial impressions. Strive to make a strong impact in successive meetings, revealing additional positive traits.

Consider these useful negotiating techniques when discussing salary. Telephone professional societies for the salary ranges of the position in your target market. Wait until the employer makes an offer. If you are asked to name your salary requirements, politely decline. You can be sure that any open position has already been budgeted. Indicate that you are considering other offers. Employers as a rule offer higher salary figures than prospective employees themselves quote. If it proves impossible to avoid the question, mention a high figure, a strong starting point for negotiation. If a salary range is mentioned, begin negotiations at the top of the scale to improve your strategic bargaining posture.

Some positions include benefits and perks. Examine carefully offers of automobile, insurance, stock options, or profit sharing. Healthy benefit packages might help compensate for low starting salaries. Beware of accepting any job offer during an initial interview. Postpone your acceptance for a few days. Take the time to compare other offers. A reasonable gestation period may influence the employer to raise the initial offer for fear of losing you. A few days or a week to consider an offer is within reason. Wait too long and you'll lose your negotiating leverage.

Salary is only one component of employment. At least as important is your opportunity to work with top creative talent in a stimulating environment. Consider the challenge of the position. Examine your chance for personal growth. Weigh your job responsibilities. Remember that most creative people make frequent job changes in their early careers. Moves are made for additional exposure, responsibility and compensation. Initially seek a challenge, and financial reward will follow.

If you are fortunate enough to find a position where your daily activities don't seem like work, then your job search will have paid rich dividends. Individuals able to give to a position more than they take from it are lucky indeed. The stimulation and satisfaction of creative work contributes immensely to your life, to the lives of your family and co-workers, and to society. If your creative resume helps you get the interview that leads to rewarding employment, then this book will have achieved its goal.

Creative
Resumes

More than eighty creative resumes are reproduced in the remainder of this book. Examine them closely. Each resume began as a dream and a blank sheet of paper. Each reflects the development of a unique idea. Some of the resumes evolved quickly, while others were born of considerable sweat and rework. Notice how every creative sample conveys a dominant "Big-Idea." Each reflects some unique trait of its designer. All of the resumes shown reach beyond the expected to stimulate an interview.

Sample resumes are grouped in order of experience. Those shown first were created to land an internship, co-op position, or summer job. Next appear resumes that were developed concurrently with visual portfolios to seek entry-level positions. Creative resumes by experienced professionals complete the selection.

Production requirements for this book necessitated showing most resumes at 85% of original size, some smaller. Resume colors, paper weight, and finish do not match up to the originals, but production credits have been included to help compensate and give valuable specifications. By viewing all the resume samples in black only, you can focus on form and content.

Examples are included for your visual stimulation. Learn from the resume samples but do not copy them. Imitation contradicts the very concept of creative resumes. Push your own resume well beyond the samples shown. Remember, it will be unique only if it mirrors your special attributes. Use the examples as visual springboards to help you design your ideal creative resume.

Resume

Michael Anthony Shea
429 West Fourth Street
Chico, California 95926

Personal

Born 11-11-60 Interests include cycling, skiing, backpacking, and calligraphy.

Education

Currently studying Graphic Design at the School of Communications at the California State University, Chico. Areas of emphasis include: Rapid Visualization, Typography, Lettering, Publication Design, Package Design, Calligraphy, Architectural Rendering, Environmental Graphics, Illustration, and Photography. Minor courses taken in Industrial Technology include: Process Camera, Offset Lithography, Screen Printing, Copy Preparation, Ink and Paper Technology.

Work/Experience

Summer 1981/1982 employed as staff artist for Time&Space Advertising in Sacramento, California. Duties included Concept development, typesetting, design and layout. Gained experience in stripping, platemaking, halftone photography, and binding/finishing at the in-house print facility.

Fall 1982 participated in the National Student Exchange. The host institution being the University of Massachusetts, Amherst. Studied Calligraphy under Wang Hui Ming.

Summer 1983 employed in Kenai, Alaska for Fisherman's Packing, Inc.

Awards

1981 Honorable Mention   PG&E Energy Conservation poster design competition.

1982 Second Award   Sacramento Chamber of Commerce Business in the Arts poster/mark competition.

1983 Honors Award   Annual juried CSUC Graphic Design Show, Publication Design.

Activities

Treasurer, Designers in Progress, 1983
Spring 1982 Attended the John Mattos Airbrush Workshop.
Spring 1984 Attended the Brian Collentine poster workshop.
Member ADAC

Design: Mike Shea
Type: Typewriter (Elite)
Ink: Black Photocopy w/Prismacolor
Paper: White Classic Laid, 20 lb.

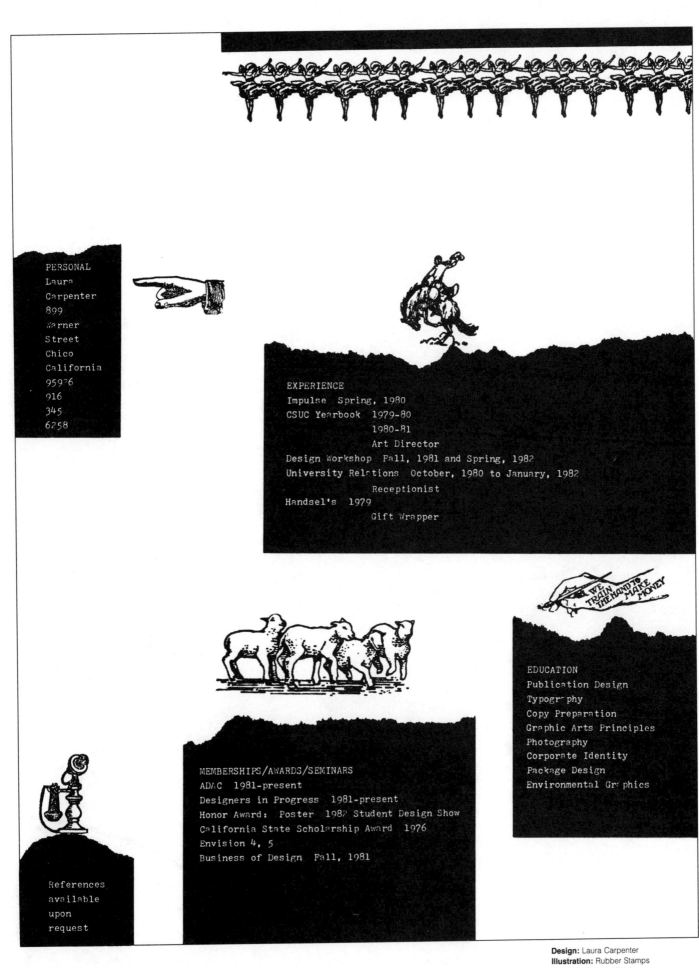

PERSONAL
Laura
Carpenter
899
Warner
Street
Chico
California
95926
916
345
6258

EXPERIENCE
Impulse Spring, 1980
CSUC Yearbook 1979-80
                1980-81
                Art Director
Design Workshop Fall, 1981 and Spring, 1982
University Relations October, 1980 to January, 1982
                Receptionist
Handsel's 1979
                Gift Wrapper

EDUCATION
Publication Design
Typography
Copy Preparation
Graphic Arts Principles
Photography
Corporate Identity
Package Design
Environmental Graphics

MEMBERSHIPS/AWARDS/SEMINARS
ADAC 1981-present
Designers in Progress 1981-present
Honor Award: Poster 1982 Student Design Show
California State Scholarship Award 1976
Envision 4, 5
Business of Design Fall, 1981

References
available
upon
request

Design: Laura Carpenter
Illustration: Rubber Stamps
Type: Typewriter (Elite)
Ink: Black Photocopy w/Multicolor Stamps
Paper: White Bond, 20 lb.

57

Résumé

Michelle M. Shibata
903 West Second Avenue #7
Chico, California
95926

Personal

Born 4-17-61
Interests: ballet, backpacking, volley-
ball and swimming

Education

Attending California State University, Chico. A VIS
COMM major in the School of Communications. Courses
completed include: Lettering, Typography, Rapid Visualization, Kinegraphics, Publication, Calligraphy, Advertising Design, Poster Design and Photography.
Other related courses include: Offset Lithography,
Screen Printing, Letterpress, Process Camera Techniques,
and Color Design.

Attended U.C. Davis for two years. General emphasis
on Drafting, Calligraphy, and Descriptive Drawing.

Work/experience

Chico State Associated Students
1982 - 1983.
Designed 1982 Renaissance Festival Poster,
1983 Student Directory, and Program Cover
as well as the Committee's T-shirts for the
Annual "Pioneer Days" event in Spring 1983.

Campus Market "5", Chico
Designed ad slick printed in the 1983
Pioneer Days Program.

Designers in Progress, Chico
Poster Design for Guest Speaker.

ELLIS Engineering, Drafting, and Art
Supplies, Chico
8/1983 to present.
Sales, Cashier. Serving students, Engineers,
and Architects in the area.

Dr. Fumio Shibata, D.D.S., San Francisco
1977 - 1982.
Dental Assistant/Receptionist.

Hungry House, San Rafael
1979 - 1982.
Waitress/Hostess.

Awards/honors

1983   Honorable Mention   Eighth Annual
                             Chico State Student Show
1983   One of Three   Lettering/Calligraphy catagory
        winners   Ad slick
                             Caribou Mountaineering
1982   First Place   Soft Luggage Manufacturer
                             1982 Pioneer Days
1981 - to present   T-shirt Design catagory
                             Dean's Honor List
                             California State University
1980 - 1981   Chico, CA
                             Dean's Honor List
                             University of California
                             Davis, CA

Activities

Member of Designers in Progress. 1982 to present.
Member of Delta Zeta Sorority. 1981 to present.
Positions held: Vice-president/Rush Chairman,
Panhellenic Delegate, Sorority Educator, and
Activities Chairman.
Spring 1984, attended Brian Collentine's Poster Design
workshop.

Design: Michelle Shibata
Type: Typewriter (Courier)
Ink: Black Photocopy w/Marker Resist.
Paper: Blueline Grid Bond, 20 lb.

RESUME

LINDA ELIZABETH CLARK

P.O. Box 549
Forest Ranch, CA
95942-0549
Phone: 916/891-5394

age: 25
marital status: single

EDUCATION

California State University, Chico
9/1979 to present
B.A. Degree in Graphic Design, in progress
Coursework completed in copy preparation,
typography, photography, packaging,
publication design, and offset lithography.

California State University, Chico
B.A. Degree in Fine Art
Graduated with Distinction
Emphasis in drawing and watercolor painting.

WORK EXPERIENCE

Quad-co Printing, Inc., Chico, CA
6/1978 to 1/1981, and 8/1981 to present
Lithographic stripper, responsible for all
film assembly and platemaking, including
four color process, in quality oriented
commercial printing company.

California State University, Chico
9/1981 to present
Graphic design intern working on University
Gallery publicity posters.

Chico News and Review, Chico, CA
7/1981 to present
Contributing designer and illustrator, and
copy camera operator for local community
newspaper.

Reber, Glenn and Marz, Advertising, Reno, NV
2/1981 to 6/1981
Fulltime internship position as graphic
designer and production artist in
advertising agency.

DesignWare, Inc., San Francisco, CA
9/1980 to 10/1980
Worked on graphic production of textbook
and workbook about computers.

Rapid Repro, Inc., Chico, CA
2/1978 to 6/1978
Responsible for all pre-press operations
(paste-up, camera, stripping, platemaking)
and ran small offset press in printing
shop.

WORKSHOPS AND SEMINARS

Albers Color Theory Workshop 11/1980
California State University, Chico

Envision 7 seminars 4/1981
Envision 6 seminars 4/1980
Art Directors and Artists Club, Sacramento

Portfolio Workshop with Michael Vanderbyle
12/1979
Art Directors and Artists Club, Sacramento

Basic Line, Halftone and PMT Techniques
10/1979
Eastman Kodak Co., San Francisco

Graphic Arts Technical Foundation seminars
9/1978 and 9/1979 So. San Francisco

MEMBERSHIPS

Art Directors and Artists Club of Sacramento
member since 1979

Superior California Club of Printing House
    Craftsmen
Member since 1979
Board of Directors 1980/1981
Newsletter Graphic Coordinator 1980/1981

Designers in Progress, CSU, Chico
member since 1979
Steering Committee 1980/1981

REFERENCES AVAILABLE ON REQUEST

59

Design: Linda Clark Johnson
Type: Typewriter (Courier)
Ink: Black Photocopy
Paper: Gray Classic Laid, 24 lb.

R   E   S   U   M   E

Tom Hermansen - Graphic Design

319 W. Frances Willard Ave.   Telephone
Chico, California   916/891-1076 home
9 5 9 2 6   916/895-5357 work

Personal		Born: August 8, 1950	Single
Education	1978 - 1980	Master of Arts expected Summer 1980 Public Communications - Graphic Design emphasis California State University, Chico	
	1974 - 1975	Standard Secondary Credential - Art California State University, Hayward	
	1971 - 1972	Bachelor of Arts - Art University of California, Davis	
	1968 - 1970	Associate of Arts - Art Diablo Valley College, Pleasant Hill, California	
Workshops	1979	Illustrators Workshop California State University, Sacramento	
	1979	Dale Carnegie Personal Improvement Course Chico, California	
	1977	Photo and Sound Company - Slide-Tape Workshop San Francisco, California	
	1976	Kodak P.M.T. and Plate-making Workshop San Francisco, California	
	1973	Nikon School of Photography San Jose, California	
	1973	Jade Fon Woo, A.W.S., Watercolor Workshop Asilomar, California	
Employment	1980	Instructor - Copy Preparation and Typography California State University, Chico	
	1979	Instructor - Copy Preparation California State University, Chico	
	1979	Graphic Designer - Image Group Design Chico, California	
	1978	Teaching Assistant - Foundation Design Class California State University, Chico	

	1978	Graphics and Darkroom Technician - Duplicating Center California State University, Chico
	1976	Teaching Assistant - Foundation Graphic Arts Class Chabot College, Hayward, California
	1975 - 1977	Head Graphic Designer - Media Services Chabot College, Hayward, California
	1975	Signs and Display - Cost Plus Imports Walnut Creek and Oakland, California
	1975	Substitute Teacher - Art San Francisco Bay Area
	1975	Summer School Teacher - Arts and Crafts Mt. Eden High, Hayward, California
	1973 - 1980	Free-lance Design
Awards	1978	"Best in Show" Graphic Design - C.I.C.S. Student Show California State University, Chico
	1978	Honor Award - Envision 4 Design Conference Davis, California
	1965	Eagle Scout Award - Boy Scouts of America Troop 212 - Moraga, California
Memberships		Art Directors and Artists Club Sacramento, California
		Designers in Progress - Student Organization California State University, Chico
		Center for Design Palo Alto, California
		Superior California Club of Printing House Craftsmen Chico, California
Interests		Calligraphy Guitar Sailing Drama
		References will be furnished upon request

Design: Tom Hermansen
Type: Typewriter (Letter Gothic)
Ink: Black Photocopy
Paper: White Bond, 20 lb.

A S P I R I N G

D E S I G N E R

P I R I G E R

D E S I G E R

Personal
Stacey E. Graffweg
120 Menlo Way #4
Chico CA. 95926 (916) 893-5629

Intent
Internship position in the field of Graphic Design.

Education
Will receive a Bachelor of Arts Degree in Visual
Communications from California State University, Chico
in May 1984.
Minor: Industrial Technology/Fine Arts
Attended the University of California, Davis 1980-81.
Educational Experience In:
Illustration Design
Publication Design
Typographic Design
Rapid Visualization
Kinegraphics
Copy Preparation

Employment
Flume Burger; Chico CA 1981-82, waitress
Knotbumper; Chester CA Summers of 1979-81, waitress
Work study for the University of California, Davis
Animal Science Department 1980-81.

**Memberships and
Interests**
Designers In Progress 1982-83
UCD Field Hockey Team 1980-81
UCD Women's Track Team 1980-81
I enjoy running and painting in my spare time.

Design: Stacey Graffweg
Type: Eras
Ink: Black w/Red Marker
Paper: White Karma, 80 lb.

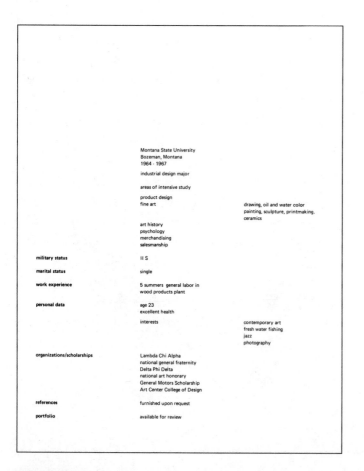

permanent address/phone	care of John Berryman 2040 Aberdeen Street Butte, Montana 59701	(406) 723-8243
degree	Bachelor of Science Degree in Industrial Design (with honors) Art Center College of Design September 25, 1970	
education	Art Center College of Design Los Angeles, California 1967 - 1970	
	product design major	
	areas of intensive study	
	product design	designed new and existing products, prepared complete formal presentations, prepared detailed engineering drawings and exploded views
	package design	redesigned existing packages, originated product names and designed logotypes, prepared 3-D package mock-ups
	graphic design	worked in two and three dimension, dealt with corporate identity and typography
	model construction	worked in plaster, automotive modeling clay, urethane foam, fiberglas, paper
		used vacuum forming machine to form styrene plastic
		worked on wood and metal lathes, drill press, band saw, and with hand tools
	rendering	worked in pencil, chalk, dri-marks, gouache, acrylic and water color
		prepared idea sketches, presentation sketches and finished renderings

	Montana State University Bozeman, Montana 1964 - 1967	
	industrial design major	
	areas of intensive study	
	product design	
	fine art	drawing, oil and water color painting, sculpture, printmaking, ceramics
	art history psychology merchandising salesmanship	
military status	II S	
marital status	single	
work experience	5 summers general labor in wood products plant	
personal data	age 23 excellent health	
	interests	contemporary art fresh water fishing jazz photography
organizations/scholarships	Lambda Chi Alpha national general fraternity Delta Phi Delta national art honorary General Motors Scholarship Art Center College of Design	
references	furnished upon request	
portfolio	available for review	

Design: David Berryman
Type: IBM Univers
Ink: Black
Paper: White Strathmore Bond

Susan Donnelly
4 Fraser Road
Westport, CT 06880
(203) 226-9914

Work Experience:
Advertising Sales & Design
(1978-1979)
Chico News & Review
Chico, CA
Dealt with client from ad concept to
finished art; initiated, maintained and
billed accounts; coordinated staff
hiring; served on management
committees; extensive use of stat
camera and Compugraphic headliner.

Editorial Cartoonist (1977)
Vidette Daily Newspaper
Illinois State University, Normal

Illustrator/Designer (1977)
"Kiss" Silkscreened T-shirts
Normal, IL

Memberships:
Art Directors & Artists Club
Sacramento, CA

Women in Communications, Inc.
Social Chairperson
Chico Chapter

Co-founded "Designers in Progress"
Student design organization, CSUC

Education:
Illinois State University, Normal
Bachelor of Arts, (Spring 1978)
Visual Communications
Emphasis: Graphic Arts, Drawing,
Painting

California State University, Chico
(Intermittent through Fall 1979)
Emphasis: Advertising, Environmental
& Package Design, Kinegraphics,
Corporate Identity & Copywriting

Workshops/Conferences
"Envision" (1978 & 1979)
Annual Western Design Conference
Sacramento, CA

The Illustrators Workshop (1979)
Sacramento, CA

Small Business Management (1979)
Chico, CA

Glass Arts Society Conference (1978)
Monterey, CA

Television Production Workshop (1977)
Normal, IL

63

Design: Susan Donnelly
Type: California
Ink: Black
Paper: White Gilbert Bond, 24 lb.

resume

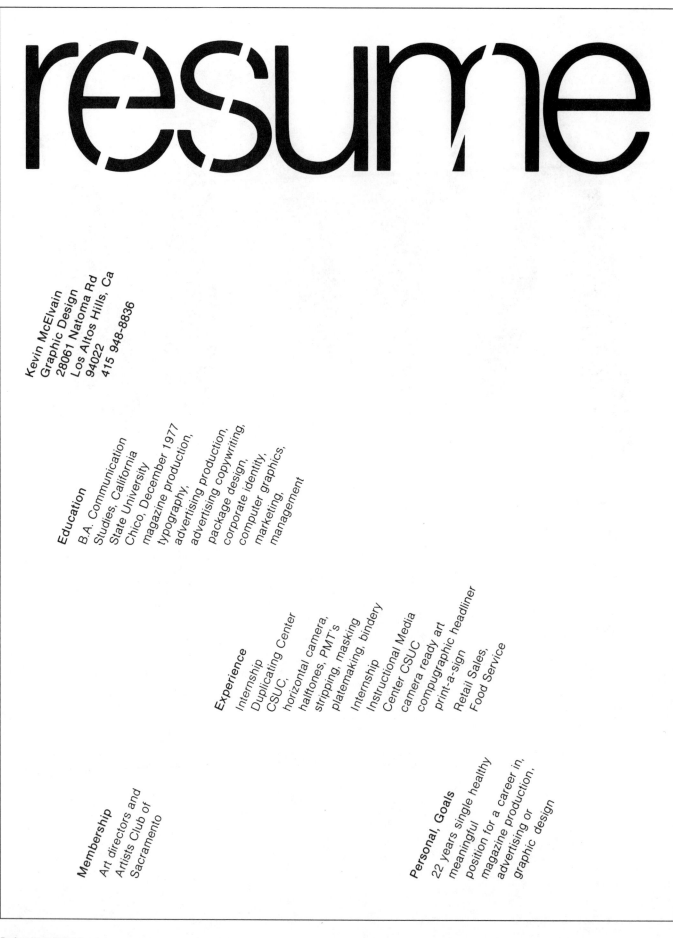

Kevin McElvain
Graphic Design
28061 Natoma Rd
Los Altos Hills, Ca
94022 415 948-8836

Education
B.A. Communication
Studies, California
State University
Chico, December 1977
magazine production,
typography,
advertising production,
advertising copywriting,
package design,
corporate identity,
computer graphics,
marketing,
management

Experience
Internship
Duplicating Center
CSUC,
horizontal camera,
halftones, PMT's
stripping, masking
platemaking, bindery

Internship
Instructional Media
Center CSUC
camera ready art
compugraphic headliner
print-a-sign

Retail Sales,
Food Service

Membership
Art directors and
Artists Club of
Sacramento

Personal, Goals
22 years single healthy
meaningful
position for a career in,
magazine production,
advertising or
graphic design

Design: Kevin McElvain
Type: Helvetica
Ink: Red
Paper: Ivory Classic Laid, 24 lb.

Sandra McHenry
(916) 342-1949

Education

1972-1974   California State University, Chico B.A. Graphic Design, Visual Communications (June 1974)

Emphasis   Packaging, corporate identity, typography, advertising, information systems, photomechanical reproduction, black and white and color photography.

1969-1972   Montana State University

Emphasis   Industrial design, interior design, graphic design, art, ceramics, drawing, painting.

Experience

1973-1974   Unique Printing and Publishing Co. Graphic Designer, Prepared camera ready art. Operated IBM typesetting machine, plate-making machine, small offset press.

1973   Brock Printing Graphic Designer, Prepared camera ready art, typesetting, dealt with special problems of book production.

Personal

Goals   Position as a graphic designer, preferably in University publications.

Interests   Enjoy tennis, photography, skiing.

Status   22 years old, single and healthy.

Design: Sandra McHenry
Type: Avant Garde
Ink: Red
Paper: White Kromekote, 8 pt.

CYNTHIA JEANE CASTALDO

ADDRESS
9493 Burns Court
Roseville, CA 95678
916 791.7544

EDUCATION
1984
B.A. Visual Communications
California State University, Chico

MAJOR EMPHASIS
Illustration
Rendering for Design
Publication Design
Corporate Identity
Lettering
Typography
Environmental Graphics
Packaging Design
Video Graphics

MINOR EMPHASIS
Photomechanical Reproduction
Copy Preparation
Photography
Advertising Copywriting
Technology of Type
Computer Graphics

WORK EXPERIENCE
1982/1984
Assistant Manager
Jiffyprint Copycenter

Customer Relations
Production Designer
Xerox 9200 Operator
Bindery Operator

1980
Photography Workshop Assistant
Yosemite National Park
Yosemite Institute

INTERNSHIP
1981
Press Operator
Duplicating Center
California State University, Chico

Operator of Multilith 2650
Paper and metal plate reproduction

ORGANIZATIONS/WORKSHOPS
Art Directors and Artist Club
of Sacramento
Envisions Seven and Ten Conference
Color Theory Workshop

REFERENCES UPON REQUEST

Design: Cynthia Castaldo
Type: Helvetica
Ink: Black, Maroon
Paper: White Karma, 80 lb.

Graphic &
Illustration
Design

David
Nickel
6738
Calle
Buena
Tucson
Arizona
85715
(602)
296
7802

JOB OBJECTIVE
To increase my knowledge and skills by getting involved in any aspect of the graphic arts trade.

EDUCATION
ARIZONA STATE UNIVERSITY, College of Fine Arts, Fall 1980 - Spring 1983. Graduated with a BFA in graphic design. Included were courses in typography, illustration, photography, serigraphy, intaglio, graphic arts techniques and processes, graphic reproduction design, ceramics, woodworking, and fine art printing.
UNIVERSITY OF COLORADO, College of Arts and Sciences, Fall 1978-Spring 1980. Included were courses in drawing, intaglio, and lithography.

WORK EXPERIENCE
POINT MAGAZINE, June 1981 - January 1982. Illustration and Advertising Design and Paste up.
GODFATHER'S PIZZA, July 1981 - June 1983. Chef and Shift Supervisor.
ECLECTIC CAFE, December - January 1980 and 1981. Chef.
TUCSON COUNTRY CLUB, Summer 1979. Chef.
HUNGRY FARMER RESTAURANT, October 1976 - May 1979. Chef and Inventory.

EXHIBITIONS AND AWARDS.
STUDENT PRINTMAKING SHOW, 1982. Harry Wood Art Gallery, Arizona State University. Two intaglio prints accepted.
STUDENT ART EXHIBIT, 1981. Matthews Center Art Gallery, Arizona State University. Juried show, intaglio print accepted.
IBM ARTS AND CRAFTS SHOW, 1981, Tucson, Arizona. Intaglio print and ink drawing accepted in Graphics Division, first place and honorable mention.
IBM ARTS AND CRAFTS SHOW, 1979, Tucson, Arizona. Intaglio print accepted in Graphics Division, first place.
INDUSTRIAL ARTS FAIR, 1978, Colorado State University. Pencil drawing and ink drawing accepted in Technical Drawing, two first places.

REFERENCES
Available upon request.

PERSONAL INFORMATION
DAVID NICKEL
6738 Calle Buena
Tucson, Arizona 85715
(602) 296-7802
Birthdate September 15, 1960
Marital Status, single

USA
20c

Design: David Nickel
Illustration: David Nickel
Type: Palatino
Ink: Four Color Process
Paper: White Kromekote, 8 pt.

K A T I E
R I C H A R D S O N

PERSONAL: Katie Richardson
Post Office Box 1028
Tahoe City, California 95730
Telephone 916. 583.4648

EDUCATION: 1984 Graduate from
California State University, Chico with a
Bachelor of Arts degree in Information
and Communication Studies with an
emphasis in Graphic Design. Course
work included: Advertising Design,
Corporate Identity, Publication Design,
Packaging, Typography, Environmental Graphics, Lettering, and
Illustration. Skills acquired in course
work included: concept development,
graphic arts photography, preparation
of camera-ready art, and type
specification.

AWARDS: 1984 Annual Design
Show, California State University, Chico,
Ca. Honor Award: Business System.
1981 PG&E Conservation Poster
Competition, Honor Award.

INTERNSHIPS/WORK EXPERIENCE: 1983
Chico News & Review, Chico, Ca.
Advertising designer. Responsibilities
included: concept development and
advertisment design, preparation of
camera-ready art including paste up,
and type specification.
1983 Construction Management
Institute, Freelance designer.
Developed corporate identity
program.
1980-1984. While attending college,
developed interpersonal communication skills with the following people-
oriented companies: Alpine
Meadows Ski Resort, and Sierra
Pacific Landscaping Co.

MEMBERSHIPS/ACTIVITIES: 1982-
1984 Designers in Progress, California
State University, Chico, Ca.
1984 Envision 10, Sacramento, Ca.

References available upon request

Design: Katie Richardson
Type: Avant Garde, Glaser Stencil Bold
Ink: Green, Purple
Paper: Karma Natural, 80 lb.

PERSONAL

Anne Marie Sheehan
1953 Vista Caudal
Newport Beach
California 92660
714-640-7028

EDUCATION

1980 Bachelor of Arts degree
Visual Communications
California State University, Chico

Courses in Corporate Identity,
Publication Design, Packaging,
Typography, Advertising
Copywriting, Environmental
Graphics, Kinegraphics, Creative
Problem Solving

EXPERIENCE

1980 vanDoorn Design
Chico, California
Graphic design and production

1980 Chico News & Review
Advertising design and production,
promotional and marketing
material. Experience with PMT
camera, Compugraphic headliner
and AM Varityper 4510.

1980 Internship
Sacramento Magazine
Advertising design and production

1979 Internship
Matt Thompson Design
Santa Rosa, California
Graphic design and production

1977 Internship
Instructional Media Center
California State University, Chico
Graphic design and production

AWARDS/MEMBERSHIPS

Sacramento Women in Advertising
Student Competition
1979 Best in Show
brochure and mark design

California State University, Chico
Student Competition
1979 Honor Award

Designers in Progress,
CSU/Chico

Sacramento Art Directors and
Artists Club

References available
upon request

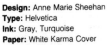
Design: Anne Marie Sheehan
Type: Helvetica
Ink: Gray, Turquoise
Paper: White Karma Cover

Resume

Alan Rellaford
Graphic Designer

Birthdate: 6.28.60

5640 Sawmill Rd.
Paradise, Ca 95969
916.877.2215

References available upon request

Education

Bachelor of Arts Degree in Visual Communication, May 1982
Minor in Graphic Arts Technology/Art
California State University, Chico

Course of Study

Corporate Identity, Packaging, Advertising Design, Advertising
Copywriting, Lettering, Kinegraphics, Illustration, Typography,
Publication Design, Photography, Advertising Production.

Employment Experience

1980-1982
Seasonal Firefighter
California Department of Forestry
1980-1982
Training Officer/Firefighter
Butte County Fire Department
1980-1981
Studio/Process Camera Technician
CSU, Chico
1980-1981
Student Custodian
Associated Students, CSU, Chico

Related Experience

1982
Director and Designer
CSU, Chico Student Design Show
1981
Graphic Design Intern
Feather River Hospital
1981
Talent and Writer
TV and Radio Public Service Announcements

Memberships

Sacramento Art Directors and Artists Club
Designers In Progress, Chico, CA · Past President

Workshops/Conferences

1980, 1981, 1982
ADAC Envision Conferences · Staff
1981, 1982
ADAC Designers Workshops · Staff
1981
ADAC Making Connections Workshop

Awards/Honors

1982
1st Place for TV Public Service Announcement
California Intercollegiate Press Association
1978
Congressional Nomination
United States Naval Academy

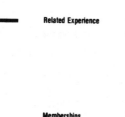

Design: Alan Rellaford
Type: Helvetica
Ink: Black
Paper: White Flokote, 70 lb.

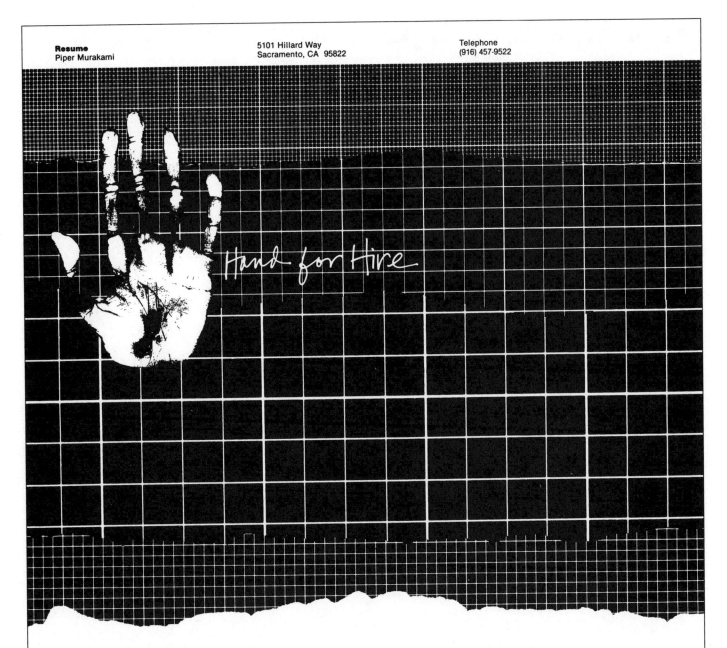

Resume
Piper Murakami

5101 Hillard Way
Sacramento, CA 95822

Telephone
(916) 457-9522

Hand for Hire

Education

California State University, Chico
Bachelor of Arts, May 1979
Graphic Design Emphasis: corporate identity, environmental graphics, packaging, publication design, television graphics, typography.

California State University, Sacramento
Intermittent through December 1977
Emphasis: illustration, screen printing, communication studies.

Sacramento City College
Associate of Arts, January 1976
Emphasis: art, graphic arts, photography.

Work Experience

Graphic Designer
Image Group, Chico
May 1979 to present

Graphic Design Intern
Image Group
January to May 1979

Yearbook Art Director/Editor
California State University, Chico
November 1978 to May 1979

Graphic Design Intern
Chico News & Review
September to December 1978

Art Director
Impulse Magazine
California State University, Chico
March to May 1978

Graphic Artist/Receptionist
State of California
Department of Health
Graphic Arts Unit
November 1975 to December 1977

Membership/Awards

Member of Art Directors and Artists Club, Sacramento

Best Visual Communicator Award, 1979
California State University, Chico

Directory Cover Competition, 1979
Art Directors and Artists Club, Sacramento

Student Show Honor Award, 1978
California State University, Chico

Interests

Photography
Illustration
Collecting children's books, various publications, and records.

Design: Piper Murakami
Type: Helvetica
Ink: Blue
Paper: White Starwhite, 80 lb.

EDUCATION

1981
B.A. in Visual Communications
California State University, Chico
Emphasis:
Corporate identity, publication design,
lettering, photography, environmental
graphics, kinegraphics, and packaging.

EXPERIENCE

1980-1981
Bob Millers Art Department; Sacramento
Graphic Designer:
Responsibilities included concept
development, client consultation,
preparation of camera-ready art, use of
stat camera.

1980-1981
University Art Gallery, Chico
Graphic Designer:
Responsibilities included poster and
collateral design for art exhibitions.

1981
University Journal
Art Director:
California State University, Chico

1979
Instructional Media Center:
C.S.U.C. Chico
Graphic Designer:
Responsibilities included concept
development, client consultation,
preparation of camera-ready art, use of
Compugraphic headliner and stat camera.

1979
Chico News and Review
Graphic Designer:
Responsibilities included design of ads
from concept to finish art, operation of
stat camera and Compugraphic headliner.

MEMBERSHIPS

ADAC, Sacramento
Designers in Progress, Chico

REFERENCES

References upon request.

AWARDS + SHOWS

1980
Best in Show
C.S.U.C. Chico Student Graphic Show

1980
One Man Photography Show:
"American Pageant"

Steve Tolleson
3329 Moorewood Ct.
Sacramento, CA. 95821
916-482-8123

T ⦾ L L E S O N

Design: Steve Tolleson
Type: Helvetica
Ink: Copper, Pink, Gray
Paper: White Karma Cover

DESIGNER FOR HIRE

Face—Belongs to **Craig Hedges**. Twenty-three years old, healthy and hard working.

Ideas—Large supply. Tend to run rampant upon release.

Old business card still in pocket—Image Group, Inc. (Chico, CA). 4/79-3/81. Conceptual design, project coordination, client consultation, copywriting and production. Also Stoner Advertising. (Enid, OK). 2/78-12/78. Conceptual design and production primarily for print advertising.

Shirt sleeves—works in them frequently.

Class ring—From California State University, Chico, Class of 1980. BA in Visual Communication. Studied advertising design, corporate identity, publications, typography, photography, copywriting, information and communication studies. Also attended Phillips University (Enid, OK). Studied Advertising design, drawing, painting, art history, and had one semester of foreign study.

No wedding ring— Just a few close calls.

Portfolio—Short but sweet. Why not take a few minutes to look at it? Craig will be calling for an appointment in a few days or you can call him at (213) 287-7488.

73

Design: Craig Hedges
Type: Futura Extra Bold, Garamond
Ink: Black
Paper: White Karma, 80 lb.

Donald Price

Advertising Design
Photography

471 East 7th Street
Chico, California 95926
(916) 343-2278

Resume

Work Experience

DESIGN/PHOTOGRAPHY: 1973 to present, Studios Grafik, 3008 Esplanade, Chico, California 95926. Designed business systems, brochures, publication covers, package labels; handled photography; worked with camera-ready art and client relations.

FREELANCE DESIGN/PHOTOGRAPHY: September 1973 to June 1974, University Relations, California State University, Chico. Did photography and designed folders, publication covers, and instructional media presentations.

PHOTOGRAPHY LABORATORY ASSISTANT: September 1973 to June 1974, California State University, Chico. Provided assistance and instruction to photography students about equipment and procedures.

FREELANCE PHOTOGRAPHY: 1971 through 1973, Penthouse Interior Decorators, 1454 Chestnut Street, Redding, California 96001. Photographed building interiors and promotional portraits.

MILITARY DUTY: June 1968 to January 1971, CAPTAIN, US Army Corps of Engineers. Received commission from the US Army Engineer Officer Candidate School. Held responsible command and staff positions in theaters of operation in the USA, Germany, and Vietnam. Received Honorable Discharge in June 1974.

MANAGER TRAINEE: 1967 to 1968, Dicker's Department Store, Redding, California. Responsibilities included sales, merchandising, and window display.

FLOOR MANAGER: 1964 to 1967, Mecca Sporting Goods, Redding, California. Responsibilities included sales, personnel supervision, merchandising, and show room display.

Education

BACHELOR OF ARTS DEGREE IN VISUAL COMMUNICATIONS: California State University, Chico, June 1974. Studied GRAPHIC DESIGN in the areas of corporate identification, packaging, advertising, typography, and camera-ready art; PHOTOGRAPHY in black and white, color, studio lighting, portraits, special effects. SPECIAL INTERESTS in television and fine art.

ASSOCIATES OF ARTS DEGREE: Shasta Junior College, Redding, California, June. Studied general education and art.

Personal Data

STATISTICS: Age 27, single, excellent health

BACKGROUND: Born and raised in Northern California. Participated in school sports and local activities.

INTERESTS: Tennis, snow skiing, hiking

References

John Gregg Berryman: Design Director for Image Group and Associate Professor at California State University, Chico, (916) 345-6564

Charles Osborn: Director of Studios Grafik, 3008 Esplanade, Chico, California 95926, (916) 345-1629

Dr. Gary Jones: Photographer for Image Group and Associate Professor at California State University, Chico, (916) 345-5216

William P. White: Associate Professor in Mass Communications at California State University, Chico. (916) 345-6216

Design: Don Price
Type: Palatino
Ink: Black w/Gray Screen
Paper: Ivory Strathmore Laid, 24 lb.

Donald Price
Graphic Design
Photography

Work Experience

Graphic Design: September 1974 to September 1975, Staff Designer, Industrial Design Affiliates, 8900 Olympic Boulevard, Beverly Hills, California 90211. Designed publication layouts and covers, information systems, advertising layouts, point of purchase displays, comprehensive art; specified type and worked extensively with paste-up and camera-ready art preparation.

Photography: July 1974 to September 1974, Official Photographer for the 1974 California State Fair, Sacramento, California. Awarded the contract to head a team of photographers that photographed for promotions, press releases, and record the events and people that participated and visited the fair activities; worked with 35mm and 2¼ x 2¼ inch cameras, portable lighting, black and white and color, quick processing methods, UPI and AP releases; extensive relations with the public and dignitaries.

Freelance Photography: 1974 to present, Gaylord Bennitt Design, 2705 K Street, Sacramento, California 95816. Product and promotional photography.

Freelance Design and Photography: 1974 to present, Image Group, 330 Flume Street, Chico, California 95926. Advertising layout, comprehensive art, promotional photography, and camera-ready art preparation.

Freelance Photography: July 1974 to September 1974, Ted Thames Design Associates, 2705 K Street, Sacramento, California 95816. Promotional and press photography.

Graphic Design and Photography: 1973 to 1974, Studios Grafik, 3008 Esplanade, Chico, California 95926. Designed business systems, brochures, publication covers, package labels; product and promotional photography; worked with camera-ready art and client relations.

Freelance Design and Photography: September 1973 to June 1974, University Relations, California State University, Chico. Designed folders, publication layouts and covers; promotional photography; instructional media presentation; portable and studio television presentation.

Photography Laboratory Assistant: September 1973 to June 1974, California State University, Chico. Provided assistance and instruction to photography students about equipment and procedures.

Freelance Photography: 1971 to 1974, Penthouse Interior Decorators, 1454 Chestnut Street, Redding, California 96001. Photographed building interiors, exteriors, and personal portraits for promotion and press release.

Education

Bachelor of Arts Degree in Visual Communications: California State University, Chico, June 1974. Studied **Graphic Design** in the areas of corporate identification, packaging, advertising, typography, and camera-ready art preparation; **Photography** in black and white, color, studio and natural lighting, various camera formats, portraits, product, environmental, architectual, special effects, materials, and processing methods; **Special Interests** in television production, art and business administration.

Associate in Arts Degree in Art: Shasta Junior College, Redding, California, June 1967. Studied general education and art.

Personal Data

Statistics: Age 29, married, excellent health

Background: Born and raised in Northern California. Participated in school sports and local activities.

Interests: Tennis, snow skiing, hiking

Military Duty: June 1968 to January 1971, Captain, US Army Corps of Engineers. Received commission from the US Army Engineer Officer Candidate School. Held responsible command and staff positions in theaters of operation in the USA, Germany, and Vietnam. Received Honorable Discharge in June 1974.

Address

5966 Raymond Way
Sacramento, California 95820
Telephone 916 457-5152

Design: Don Price
Type: Helvetica
Ink: Black, Gray
Paper: White Strathmore Cover

Chuck Haines

Experience

1983
Graphic Design Intern
Instructional Media Center
CSU Chico
Responsibilities: Client Relations,
Design and Production of Posters,
Brochures, Flyers, Publications,
Technical Charts and Graphs.
Operated Compugraphic Headliner,
Vertical Camera, Dubner CBG1
Graphic Generating Computer.

1981/1983
Grocery Clerk
Lucky Supermarkets
Davis/Chico, California

1980/1981
Designer/Illustrator
Rodney Design
Responsibilities: Design, Production,
Client Relations, Illustration,
Bookkeeping, Printing Quality Control.
Operated Vertical Camera,
Compugraphic Typesetter.

1979
Library Assistant
UC Davis

Education

1982/1983
Intensive Graphic Design Curriculum
CSU Chico
Emphasis: Packaging, Environmental
Graphics, Corporate Identity,
Publication Design, Kinegraphics,
Photography, Illustration, Marketing,
Creative Problem Solving.

1979
BS Medical Illustration
UC Davis
Emphasis: Illustration, Airbrush, Life
Drawing, Watercolor, Anatomy,
Physiology, Zoology, Embryology,
Entomology, Osteotomy, Epidemiology,
Biology.

1974/1975
Orange Coast College
Costa Mesa, California

Personal

Chuck Haines
800 Arthur Street
Davis, CA 95616
916 758 1065
916 894 0153

Activities

1983
Designers in Progress
Vice President

1983
Advertising Agency Seminar
SF Art Directors Club

1983
First Place, Poster Design
Annual Juried Show
CSU Chico

1982
Cash Award
Logo Application
The Library Connection

References on Request

Design: Chuck Haines
Type: Helvetica
Ink: Black Photocopy w/Prismacolor
Paper: White Bond, 20 lb.

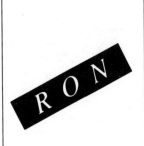

R O N

Born: August 2, 1958
Marital Status: Single

Education

*Bachelor of Arts, Visual
Communications
California State University,
Chico 1981
Studies: corporate identity,
publication design, typography,
kinegraphics, advertising
design, packaging, photography,
and copywriting.*

*Associate of Arts, Fine Art
Modesto Community College
1978
Studies: drawing, printmaking,
art history, and cartooning.*

Work Experience

*Graphic Design Intern
KVIE Channel 6
Sacramento, CA. 1981
Responsibilities: poster design,
television graphics, label
design, and paste-up. Gained
experience with vertical copy
camera and Kroy headliner.*

*Graphic Arts Intern
Kopy Kat
California State University,
Chico 1981
Responsibilities: paste-up,
stripping, and binding. Gained
experience with horizontal copy
camera and AB Dick 360 offset
press.*

*Silk Screen Artist
The Jock Shop
Chico, CA. 1980
Responsibilities: preparing black
and white art, screen
preparation, and printing one
color uniforms.*

*Salesman/Cashier
Lacques Sport Shop
Modesto, CA. 1975-1982,
intermittent
Responsibilities: sales, writing
stock orders, and pricing
merchandise.*

Workshops/Conferences

*Color Separation Workshop
Sacramento, CA. 1982
Envision
Sacramento, CA. 1980 & 1981
Color Theory Workshop
Chico, CA. 1980
Paper Making Workshop
Modesto, CA. 1978*

Memberships

*Art Directors and Artists Club
Sacramento, CA.
Designers in Progress
Chico, CA.*

*References available upon
request.*

*2725 La Palma Dr.
Modesto, CA. 95351
Phone: 209 527 0244*

Design: Ron Kirk
Type: Times Roman
Ink: Black
Paper: White Karma Cover

David E. Bacigalupi
Graphic Design

56 Alder Avenue
San Anselmo, California
94960
(415) 456-0791

Personal

Single
23 Years Old
Excellent Health

Education

Bachelor of Arts Degree
Visual Communications
California State
University, Chico
June, 1974

Studies in graphic
design with emphasis on
packaging, advertising,
corporate identity,
environmental design,
typography,
and photography.

Work Experience

Draftsman
Plant Operation,
Design Section,
California State
University, Chico

Architectural drafting,
environmental signage,
and supergraphics.

Instructor
Magazine Production,
Center for Information
and Communications
Studies,
California State
University, Chico

Instruction in magazine
design, lay out,
specification,
and production of the
campus magazine,
"Impulse."

Graphic Designer
Image Group
330 Flume Street, Chico

Preparation of camera
ready art for
advertising, packaging,
and small business
identity systems.

Graphic Designer
Free Lance

Planning and design of
corporate identity
systems, personal
identity systems,
advertising, signage,
media design, and
publication design.

Design: David Bacigalupi
Type: Korinna
Ink: Dark Brown
Paper: Gray Strathmore text, 70 lb.

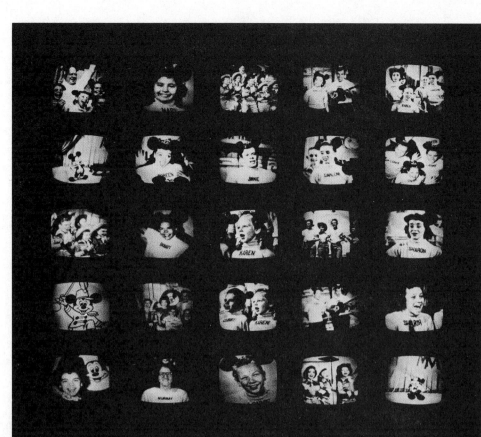

Personal

1954
With mesmorized eyes, turned
to television for an overview of the
culture, via the "Mickey Mouse Club."

1974
Twenty years later, with a new
awareness, returned to television to
explore the realities of the medium.

Experience

1975-1977
Employment at Television Services,
Instructional Media Center,
California State University, Chico;

Involved in production in over 100
programs at Chico States new multi-
million dollar color television facility.
This included creative and technical
experience in the following areas of
production: Camera operator, lighting, video tech, producer, director,
ENG operator, VTR, satellite recep-
tion, audio, technical director, floor
director, set design, and production
assistant.

The programs were both instructional materials for the University and
programs for general broadcast via
the University's television affiliate
KIXE Channel 9, a Public Broadcasting station. Also, as a part of this
experience was a rigorous mobile
production schedule using the
University's "Studio Equipped" color
van.

1976-1977
Media Prepartation Lab,
Instructional Media Center,

Assisted students and faculty with the
preparation of mediated materials including: video, film (super 8 and
16mm), slide/tape, graphics for video
and film, and still photography. Also
included was film animation and film
soundtrack recording.

Education

1973-1977
Bachelor of Arts Degree;
Center for Information and Communi-
cation Studies, California State
University, Chico.

Emphasis in Broadcasting
Cluster minor in English

1974-1977
Self supporting through
three years of college.

Recognition Awards: First prize
winner; Annual University Student
Film Awards

References available on request

Short video tape portfolio available
on request

Murray F. Cohen
10652 Larry Drive
Anaheim, California 92804
Phone: 714-535-8512
Position Desired: Production
Assistant; Writer/Researcher for
television and/or film

Design: Brian Collentine
Type: Helvetica
Ink: Black
Paper: Black & White, 70 lb.

JENNIFER
CASEY
KNOWLES

268 North Sacramento St.
Willows, CA 95988
916/934-4329

OBJECTIVE

To obtain an entry level position which will allow me to utilize my skills in working with the media and knowledge of mass communications.

EDUCATION

California State University, Chico
Bachelor of Arts,
December 1982
Major—
School of Communications, Emphasis in Public Relations
Minor—
Business Administration

PROFESSIONAL EXPERIENCE

P.R. Intern
Warrens Public Relations Associates
Chico, CA
September 1982 - December 1982
Hands on experience in working with various accounts. Developed and implemented marketing plan for a children's book, worked on promotions for a women's retail shop.

P.R. Intern
Children's Home Society of California
Chico, CA
February 1982 - May 1982
Worked on Campaign for Children, writing press releases and putting together a booklet for distribution to CHS auxiliaries throughout Northern California.

Willows Press,
Valley West Newspapers
Willows, CA
June 1980 - August 1980
Gained first hand experience in all aspects of newspaper operations with emphasis on advertising sales, writing feature stories and general news, photography, layout and pasteup.

WORK EXPERIENCE

Keno Runner
Harrah's Club
South Lake Tahoe, NV
June 1982 - August 1982
June 1981 - August 1981
Duties included extensive customer relations, and handling large amounts of cash in a busy work environment.

ACTIVITIES

Delta Zeta Sorority 4 years:
Scholarship Chairperson
Philanthropy Chairperson
Delta Sigma Pi Rose Candidate
Formal Dinner/Dance Chairperson 2 semesters

National Student Exchange Program
Fall 1980
North Carolina State University

Deans Honor List
Spring 1982

Women in Communications Inc.

REFERENCES

Marilyn Warrens
President
Warrens Public Relations Associates
430 Broadway
Chico, CA 95926
work 916/345-7673
home 916/342-6731

Marilyn Baker
Editor/Writer
Willows Press/
Willows Daily Journal
304 S. Merrill St.
Willows, CA 95988
work 916/934-5411
home 916/934-4071

John Gregg Berryman
School of Communications
California State University, Chico
Chico, CA 95929
work 916/895-6872
home 916/343-6500

Jennifer Casey Knowles

80

Design: Linda Clark Johnson
Type: Helvetica
Ink: Black, Rose Red
Paper: Ivory Classic Laid, 24 lb.

Experience

corporate identity, advertising
design, packaging, publication
design, marketing concepts.

Employment

SPRING 1981
ENTREPRENEUR of FOCAL POINT
Design, packaging, marketing, and
promotion of graphic arts materials
needed by Chico design students.

JUNE 1980 - APRIL 1981
CALIFORNIA ENERGY COMMISSION
Dealt with commissioners and staff
interpreting technical research data
relating to energy. Designed
maps for preliminary and bieniel
reports and promotional brochures.

JANUARY 1980 - APRIL 1980
COMMUNICATION DESIGN
Layout, paste up, camera work for
large G.E. technical manual.

JULY 1979 - DECEMBER 1980
OBSERVER NEWSPAPER
Advertising concept, design, layout,
camera work for weekly newspaper.

SEPTEMBER 1974 - JUNE 1975
CALIFORNIA STATE PRINTER
An internship which gave me a
thorough introduction to all
phases of the printing process.

Education

Bachelor of Arts
Visual Communications
Chico State University, 1981

Affilliation

Art Directors and Artists Club
Marketing Club, CSUC
Designers in Progress, CSUC

Cathy Holt

GRAPHIC DESIGNER
2742 Land Park Dr.
Sacramento, California 95818
(916) 442-8797

Design: Cathy Holt
Type: Helvetica
Ink: Blue-Green
Paper: White Starwhite, 70 lb.

Jennifer Victoria Cohen
8440-R Via Mallorca
La Jolla, CA. 92037
714•452•5648 or 714•455•1355

Born: June 1, 1957
Health: Excellent
Single and willing to relocate

Jennifer cohen

Professional Objective:
To obtain a competitive position relating to my fields of study, and to gain additional business experience and knowledge necessary for advancement.

Education:
Bachelor of Science: Marketing Option
California State University, Chico. Spring 1980.
Studies included: retailing, sales management, advertising, transportation and international marketing.

California Polytechnic State University, San Luis Obispo.
Spring 1977.
Studies included: textile science, special fabrics, flat pattern, advanced clothing construction and tailoring.

Secretary, Marketing Club. CSU/Chico.

Work Experience:
Assistant Manager, Zeilder & Zeilder
La Jolla, CA. July 1980 to present.
Responsibilities included opening and closing store, scheduling, general daily bookkeeping, deposits, sales and displays.

The Clothesline, Chico, CA. Spring 1979.
Responsibilities included assisting in buying inventory through jobbers in San Francisco.

United Sporting Goods, San Bruno, CA. Fall 1979.
Responsibilities included office management, bookkeeping, inventory control, deposits, payroll and scheduling.

Casual Corner, San Francisco, CA. March 1977 - Sept. 1977.
Responsibilities included retail sales with hourly quota.

Mervyn's, Daly City and Millbrae, CA. Sept. 1973 - Sept. 1975.
Responsibilities included retail sales, stocking shelves, inventory control, opening and closing registers.

Earned 100% of college expenses.

References:
Dr. Albert Long
90 Mt. Spring Ct.
San Francisco, CA.
415•566•6275

Mr. Stan Marblestone
District Manager Mervyn's
855 Broadway
Millbrae, CA.
415•692•4490

Mr. Bruce Rowan
Registrar
CSU/Chico
916•895•5142

Design: Mark Ulriksen
Type: Helvetica
Ink: Gray
Paper: Ivory Strathmore Writing, 24 lb.

82

Education

California State University, Chico, California,
Center for Information and Communication Studies,
Visual Communication, 1977 to 1979. (Black
and white and colour photography, publication
design, copywriting, corporate identity, typography,
packaging, kinegraphics, environmental graphics)

Master of Arts, University of Hawaii, Honolulu,
Hawaii, Department of Communications, 1972.
(Cross-cultural and group dynamics)

Bachelor of Arts, Pennsylvania State University,
University Park, Pennsylvania, College of Liberal
Arts, 1970.

**Margie Etta
Michelson**

67 Brookwood #22
Orinda, CA 94563
415 • 254 • 7097

Born: July 14, 1946
Height: 5'2"
Weight: 118 lbs.
Health: Excellent

Achievements

Photography exhibit, *Fruits of Our Labour*,
held at La Salles, Chico, Summer 1979.
A documentary photo exhibit of blue collar
workers in fruit and vegetable produce
yards.

Center for Information and Communication
Studies Student Show, Spring 1979.
Photography and design selected for
exhibit in a juried student visual
communication show.

Roots of Design, California State University,
Chico, Spring 1978. Assembled a slide
learning package for the Visual
Communication curriculum.

Member of ADAC, Art Directors and Artists
Club of Sacramento, 1977 to present.
This year I was part of a team to photograph
the 1979 Envision design conference.

Work Experience

Freelance graphic designer and photographer, 1977 to
present. I designed business systems, brochures, a
journal, and provided photography for attorney cases,
a fashion show and portraits.

Internship in graphic design, Instructional Media Center,
California State University, Chico, Spring semester,
1979. Designed printed pieces for clients within the
university.

Graphic designer, Office of Business and Economic
Affairs, California State University, Chico, October 1978 to
February 1979. I designed *The Northern California
Review,* a journal for the northern California business
community.

Graphic assistant, Aerospace Educational Services
Project, NASA, California State University, Chico, January
1978 to November 1978. I designed and produced
identification signage for the NASA space flight centers,
illustrations and brochures.

Photographer, Admissions Office, Student Learning
Center, and Associated Students, California State
University, Chico, Summer 1977 to Fall 1978. I did
photography for university publications, and a colour slide
production for student recruitment.

I have eight years experience in the following capacities: writing proposals and developing
academic programs; instructing students in interpersonal communication, small group
discussion and rhetoric; supervising a staff of Resident Hall Advisors (RAs); tutoring
English in an Educational Opportunity Program; supervising smoking control clinics;
coordinating and evaluating research for a community based youth project; counselling
youth and families in a delinquency diversion program.

Interests

Photography
Yoga
Writing
Swimming
Bicycling
Creative cooking
Painting

References
furnished upon
request.

Design: Malka Michelson
Type: Helvetica
Ink: Blue
Paper: White Karma, 80 lb.

Thomas **WALKER**
5 3 4 0 Harrison Rd
P a r a d i s e
Ca 95969
916/877 **6620**

EDUCATION

1980
B.A. with honors,
Visual Communication
California State University, Chico

Studies included publication
design, corporate identity,
photography, film, advertising
design, packaging, and
copywriting.

INTERNSHIPS

1980-81
Feather River Hospital
Community Relations Dept.
Paradise, CA
Graphic Designer;
Responsible for publication and
advertising design, photography,
and copywriting.

1979-80
Chico News & Review
Chico, CA
Graphic Designer;
Responsible for advertising
design and editorial layout.
Experience with stat camera,
Compugraphic headliner and AM
Varityper 4510.

1979
NASA-Ames Research Center
Phototechnical Branch
Moffett Field, CA
Photographer;
Included use of 35mm, 2¼ x 2¼,
4x5, and 8x10 cameras for
scientific and industrial
photography in studio
and on location.

WORK EXPERIENCE

1980-81
California Energy Commission
Sacramento, CA
Asst. Art Director and
Photo Editor, Biennial Report;
Responsibilities included
research, photography, editorial
design, chart and map design,
and supervision of printing.

1976-78
Council on
Int'l Educational Exchange
Los Gatos, CA
Director of Student Travel
Services, CSU, Chico;
Responsibilities included
advertising, public relations,
sales and creation of multimedia
presentations.

MEMBERSHIPS

1979-81
Art Directors and Artists Club
Sacramento, CA

1979-80
Designers in Progress
CSU, Chico
Founder and Chairman

1981
Friends of Photography
Carmel, CA

Design: Tom Walker
Type: Helvetica
Ink: Black, Green
Paper: White Kromekote Cover, 8 pt.

J   A   N   E   T   BEISSER

DESIGNER

1691 MESA DRIVE T16
SANTA ANA, CALIFORNIA 92707
714 545 3580

EDUCATION

Bachelor of Arts, Visual Communication 1982
California State University, Chico
(Corporate Identification, Publication Design,
Package Design, Advertising Design,
Typography, Photography, Illustration,
Kinegraphics)

Bachelor of Arts, Art 1978
California State University, Chico
(Drawing, Ceramics, Glass)

Rio Hondo College 1975
(Drawing, Painting, Photography)

EXPERIENCE

Warner Associates 1981
Design, Layout, Pasteup
San Diego, California

Wilson Frank Associates
Freelance Design
San Diego, California

Non Related Experience
Almond Tree 1979
Food Service
Chico, California

Carmel Valley Tennis Camp 1978
Recreation Director
Carmel Valley, California

Mill Creek Stained Glass 1977
Stained Glass Window Design
Chico, California

ACTIVITIES

Braun's Young Designer
National Competition
Package Design
Certificate of Merit

Fine Art Show
Rio Hondo College
Art Scholarship

Art Directors and
Artists Club Member
Sacramento, California

REFERENCES

upon
request

Design: Janet Beisser
Type: Helvetica
Ink: Plum
Paper: Karma Natural, 80 lb.

TIMOTHY ASPINALL. **CARMICHAEL, CA.** **3831 MISSION AVE.** **(916) 487-1145**

ACTIVITIES

Art Directors and Artist Club of Sacramento

Designers in Progress CSU/Chico Treasurer — 1981, 1982

Chalcedon Conference on the Media and the Arts Sacramento, CA 1983

Envision Design Conference Sacramento, CA 1981, 1982

AWARDS

1982 Annual Design Show CSU/Chico Honor Award: Illustration

1981 CIPA Award Impulse Magazine

1981 Annual Design Show CSU/Chico Honor Award: Publication Design Honor Award: Package Design

EDUCATION

California State University, Chico Fall 1979 to Spring 1982 B.A. Visual Communications Instructors: Gregg Berryman, George Turnbull, Gaylord Bennitt

American River College Carmichael, CA Fall 1976 to Spring 1979 A.A. Art Instructor: Gary Pruner

APPLICABLE COURSES:

Publication Design
Illustration Design
Advertising Design
Kinegraphics
Package Design
Corporate Identity
Photomechanical Reproduction
Copy Preparation
Advertising Copywriting

EXPERIENCE

Timothy Aspinall Design and Illustration Chico, CA 1983 to Present Clients: KHSL TV 12, Marilyn Warrens Public Relations, Butte Community Action Agency, The Ostomy Center Responsibilities: Identity systems, marks, advertising design, sign painting, airport displays.

Chico Times — Weekly Tabloid Chico, CA Fall 1983 — Staff Designer April 1983 — Advertising Manager, Staff Designer 1982 — Production Manager, Staff Designer Responsibilities: Editorial and advertising design, oversee production of the paper and production staff, oversee reorganization of Advertising/ Sales dept., operated Pos 1 stat camera.

KXTV Channel 10 (CBS) Sacramento, CA 1980 Internship Responsibilities: Sales promotion graphics, on-air graphics and promotional collateral, operated Compu-writer typesetter and POS 1 stat camera.

California Dept. of Forestry Ione, CA 1977 — Illustrator Responsibilities: Training manual illustrations, charts, graphs and signs.

REFERENCES

Gaylord Bennitt Art Director Girvin, Conrad & Girvin (916) 985-6600 The Bennitt Group (916) 441-0436

Gregg Berryman Instructor, Visual Communications California State University, Chico. (916) 895-6872, 343-6500

Pastor Bob Sprague Neighborhood Church Chico, CA (916) 343-6006

Kim Weir Writer, Former Editor of Chico Times Chico, CA (916) 345-5711, 893-4410

Design: Tim Aspinall
Type: Helvetica
Ink: Black, Green
Paper: White Karma Cover

RICK WONG ■ 1779 Woodland Avenue,
apt. 4, Palo Alto, California 94303 ■
EXPERIENCE ■ Design and Production,
Russell Leong Design, October 1981 to
April 1983 ■ Layout and Production,
Runner's World Magazine, June 1981 to
September 1981 ■ Design and Produc-
tion, Mabi Label Company, January 1981 to
June 1981 ■ EDUCATION ■ BS degree
in Graphic Design, San Jose State
University, September 1979 to December
1981 ■ AA degree in Architecture, City
College of San Francisco, September 1975
to May 1979 ■ References upon request

RICK WONG
415 326-7902

87

Design: Rick Wong
Type: Helvetica
Ink: Gray, Yellow
Paper: White Karma, 80 lb.

K A T H L E E N **FAIN**

D E S I G N ♆ I L L U S T R A T I O N

E D U C A T I O N

Bachelor of Arts, *Visual Communication, California State University, Chico.*
Studies included Typography, Illustration, Corporate Identification, Publication Design, Advertising Design, Photography and Kinegraphics.
Cluster Minor in Art and Industrial Technology (printing).

E X P E R I E N C E

Chico News & Review, 1981-83. Weekly news magazine, circulation 29,000. From 1981-82, was a principal staff designer responsible for the design and production of editorial content. Duties included illustration and some art direction.
From 1981-82, was member of Advertising Design staff, duties included advertising and some editorial concept development, preparation of camera-ready art and illustration. Became familiar with the use of horizontal process camera.
Camel Studios, 1891-83. Freelance Design. Designed and produced business systems, logos, invitations, menus, radio program guides and show cards for various clients.
California State University, Chico, 1980-81. Lab Assistant for Graphic Design department. Duties included care of process camera, typositor and darkroom. Also aided and instructed students in the use of equipment.

I N T E R N S H I P S & W O R K S H O P S

Chico News & Review, Summer 1980. Internship, designed and produced ads and some editorial layout.
Color Theory workshop by Gwen Amos. 1980, focused on the theory and application of color.
Impulse Magazine, Spring Semester, 1982. A magazine produced annually by the Communications Department at California State University, Chico. Acted as co-art director. Responsibilities included editorial and cover design.
Experimental Typography workshop with Gwen Amos, Fall Semester, 1982.
Class focused on the theory and design of type, including application.

R E F E R E N C E S

Available on request.

A D D R E S S

165 Kenwood Way, San Francisco, CA 94127.

T E L E P H O N E

(415) 589-2993.

Design: Kathy Fain
Type: Helvetica
Ink: Gray, Salmon, Light Green
Paper: White Moistrite Matte. 60 lb.

Karen A. Fenlon

929 West Fourth Avenue
Chico, California 95926

Telephone (916) 345-4028

Resume

Membership/Awards

Education

Employment

1977-1979
Art Directors
of Sacramento

Board of Governors
Scholarship 1977-1978

Ted Richardson
Scholarship 1978-1979

Honor Award in
Photography
Student Show 1978

1978-Present
California State
University, Chico
Graduate Studies
Emphasis
Visual communications,
corporate identity,
packaging, environmental
graphics, and creative
problem solving

1974-1978
California State
University, Chico
B.A. Art
Emphasis
Drawing, photography,
design with a minor in
Anthropology

1972-1974
Victor Valley College
Victorville, California
A.S. General Studies
Emphasis
Health Sciences
Completion of two year
program in Respiratory
Therapy

1977-1979
Instructional Media Center
Graphics/Photography
Studio
California State
University, Chico
Graphic Designer for
University faculty and staff
publications

Responsibilities included
consultation with clients,
concept development,
preparation of camera-
ready art, use of
Compugraphic headliner,
stat camera, and
photographic darkroom
equipment

1977-1979
Graphic Designer for
Performing Arts programs

Responsibilities included
coordination of program
copy, design, and
preparation of camera-
ready art.

1974-1977
CSUS Speech/Drama
Department
Properties Manager

Responsibilities included
directing crews and
coordinating stage props
for Speech/Drama and
Music productions
Poster Design

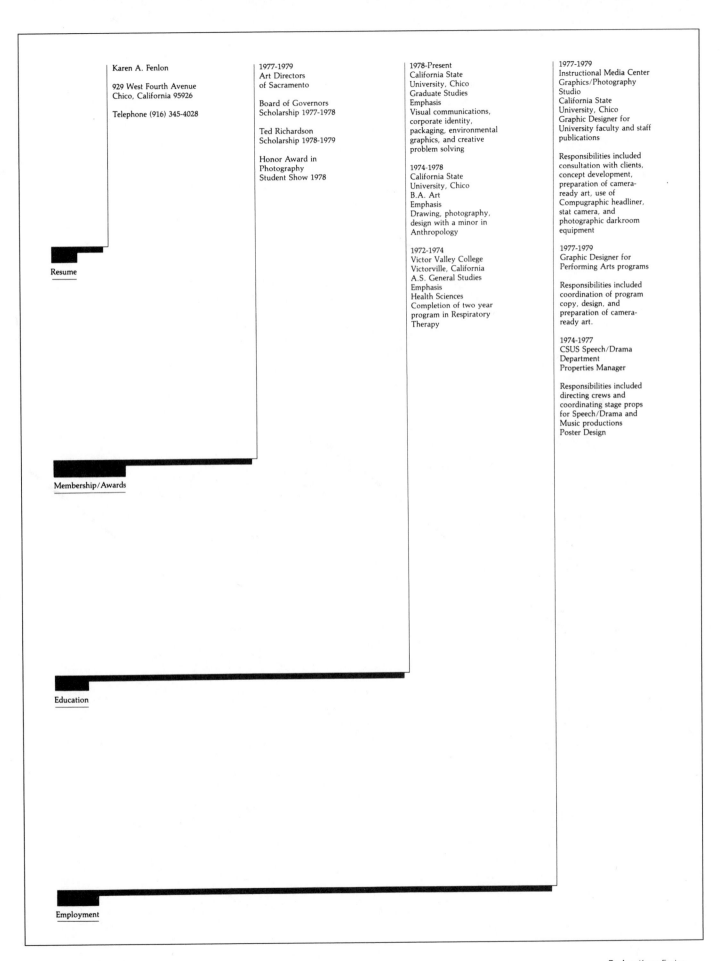

89

Design: Karen Fenlon
Type: Palatino
Ink: Maroon
Paper: White Karma Cover

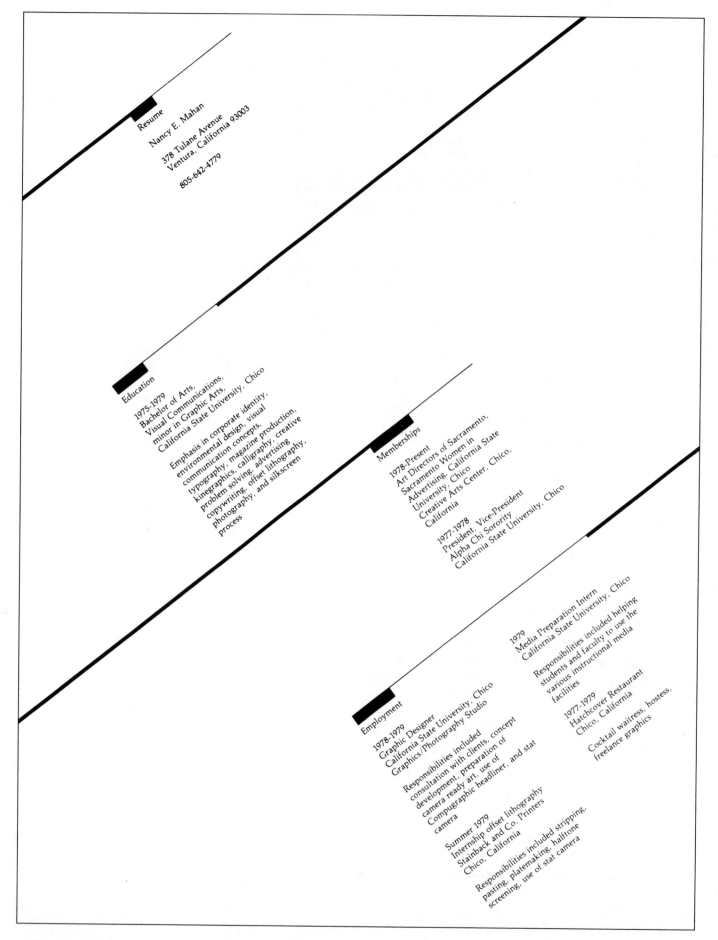

Resume

Nancy E. Mahan

378 Tulane Avenue
Ventura, California 93003

805-642-4779

Education

1975-1979
Bachelor of Arts,
Visual Communications,
minor in Graphic Arts,
California State University, Chico

Emphasis in corporate identity,
environmental design, visual
communication concepts,
typography, magazine production,
kinegraphics, calligraphy, creative
problem solving, advertising
copywriting, offset lithography,
photography, and silkscreen
process

Memberships

1978-Present
Art Directors of Sacramento,
Sacramento Women in
Advertising, California State
University, Chico
Creative Arts Center, Chico,
California

1977-1978
President, Vice-President
Alpha Chi Sorority
California State University, Chico

Employment

1978-1979
Graphic Designer
California State University, Chico
Graphics/Photography Studio

Responsibilities included
consultation with clients, concept
development, preparation of
camera ready art, use of
Compugraphic headliner, and stat
camera

Summer 1979
Internship offset lithography
Stainback and Co. Printers
Chico, California

Responsibilities included stripping,
pasting, platemaking, halftone
screening, use of stat camera

1979
Media Preparation Intern
California State University, Chico

Responsibilities included helping
students and faculty to use the
various instructional media
facilities

1977-1979
Hatchcover Restaurant
Chico, California

Cocktail waitress, hostess,
freelance graphics

Design: Nancy Mahan Swanson
Type: Palatino
Ink: Dark Green
Paper: White Karma, 80 lb.

● Resume

● Education

● Employment

● Memberships/Awards

● Abigail Stone

● 365 Lincoln Avenue
Palo Alto, California 94301

● Telephone (415) 322-2400

● 1974 - 1979
California State
University, Chico
Bachelor of Arts,
Art

Studies included
advertising design,
corporate identity,
illustration, packaging,
typography, and
● painting

● 1978 - 1979
Graphic Designer
California State
University, Chico
Graphics/Photography
Studio

Responsibilities included
concept development,
client consultation,
preparation of
camera-ready art,
use of Compugraphic
headliner and stat camera

1975 - 1978
Properties Manager,
Stage Technician
California State
University, Chico
Speech and Drama
Department

Responsibilities included
poster design, construction
of stage props, and
● supervision of stage crews

● 1978 - Present
Art Directors of
Sacramento membership

Honor Award in
Graphics,
Student Show 1978
California State
● University, Chico

●   ●   ●

91

Design: Abbi Stone
Type: Palatino
Ink: Maroon
Paper: White Karma, 80 lb.

R E S U M E

◆ Jacqueline Miller

E D U C A T I O N

81 **Bachelor of Arts**
Visual Communications
California State University, Chico
Emphasis: Advertising Design,
Publication Design, Corporate
Identification, Typography,
Copy Preparation, Environmental
Graphics, Kinegraphics,
Package Design

81 **Member of Designers in Progress**
California State University, Chico
(secretary)

E X P E R I E N C E

82 **Chico News & Review**
Graphic Designer
Responsibilities included ad
concept development,
preparation of camera-ready art,
use of stat camera

81 **Impulse Magazine**
California State University, Chico
Art Director

80 **Howard Visuals**
Graphic Designer
Responsibilities included concept
development, client consultation,
preparation of camera-ready art,
use of stat camera

80 **Instructional Media Center**
California State University, Chico
Graphic Designer, Intern
Responsibilities included concept
development, preparation of
camera-ready art, use of
Compugraphic Headliner and
stat camera

79 **Postal Instant Press**
Production
Responsibilities included
preparation of camera-ready art

(9 1 6) 8 9 1 - 0 6 1 7

◆ Rt. 4, Box 422H
Chico, CA 95926

◆ References available upon request

Design: Jacque Miller
Type: Kabel
Ink: Gray
Paper: Karma Natural Cover

R E S U M E´

PERSONAL

Larry V. Will
681 South Tustin Avenue
Suite 111
Orange, California 92666
(714) 538-0310

EDUCATION

Associated Arts Degree
Cerritos College, Norwalk

Bachelor of Fine Arts Degree
Visual Communications
Major
California State University,
Long Beach

EXHIBITS/AWARDS

Young Designers Competition
C. Braun Company
Certificate of Merit

National Paper Box
Association
Rigid Box Design
Competition
First Place Award

31st Annual Art Directors
Club of Los Angeles Show of
Advertising and Design In the
West 1976 Distinctive Bullet
Award

Departmental Scholarship
1976
California State University,
Long Beach

Departmental Award 1974
Cerritos College, Norwalk

Cerritos College Annual
Student Art Exhibit, 1975
First Place Award

Cerritos College Annual
Student Art Exhibit 1974
First Place Award

Desireé

EXPERIENCE·

Gallery Assistant
Cerritos College, Norwalk
Director: Gilbert Steel

As assistant I constructed
installations which were used
for exhibits. Also helped
organize the design of the
exhibits which included placement of lighting, color coordination, and displaying of
type.

Tiffany

Staff Artist
Cerritos College, Norwalk
Publications Director:
Jay Malinowski

While attending Cerritos I
started in the publications
department as an assistant to
the staff artist. When he left
his position, until placement
was made, I took over the
duties of staff artist. In this
position I was involved in
most of the campus printed
material for community and
campus programs. Duties
included concept direction for
all art work, full production
coordination, including camera involvement for reproduction purpose, and press
checking for quality control
of printing.

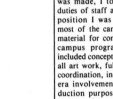

Production/Layout Person
Martin Wayne Advertising
3270 Cherry Avenue
Long Beach, California 90807

While attending CSULB I
worked part time for Martin
Wayne as a production and
layout person. Most of the
job material I worked on was
collateral for clients such as,
Long Beach Gas Co., Riccar
International, and the Bragg
Co. My duties varied accord-
ing to individual job involvement, from doing complete
production to layout and
design.

LINDSAY

FREELANCE DESIGN

During my senior year at
CSULB I contacted a com-
pany regarding some design
work. I ended up totally
designing a complete visual
communications package.
This package included a company identity for stationary,
packaging, and signage. Since
graduating from CSULB I
have continued to keep this
company as a client and have
used my professional services
to fill their visual marketing
needs.

 UNITED MEDICAL SYSTEMS

REFERENCES

George Turnbull
Professor
Center for Information and
Communicational Studies
California State University
Chico
Chico, California 95929

Jim VanEimeren
Professor
Visual Communications for
Design
California State University,
Long Beach
(213) 498-4361 or
(714) 962-9836

Jay Malinowski
Director of Publications
Cerritos College, Norwalk
(213) 860-2451 Ext. 215/216

Richard Jacks
215 Riverside Avenue
Newport Beach, California
92663
(714) 645-1550

93

Design: Larry Will
Type: Benguiat, Times Roman
Ink: Black
Paper: Gray Cambric Linen, 20 lb.

ELIZABETH M. MEKJAVICH

2325 T Street, Apt. E

RESUME

Sacramento, California 95816

916.456.9596

EDUCATION

CALIFORNIA STATE UNIVERSITY, CHICO. 1980 to 1983

WORK EXPERIENCE AND INTERNSHIPS

Bachelor of Arts with Honors in Visual Communication

INTERIOR DESIGNER, SALESPERSON, Scofield's Furniture Co.

Minor in Psychology

Sacramento, CA. 1979 to present

Emphasis in Publication, Corporate Identity, Advertising,

LITHOGRAPHIC STRIPPER, PRODUCTION ARTIST, CAMERA OPERATOR,

Typography, Packaging, and Calligraphy.

Quadco Printing Inc. Chico, CA. Summer 1983

CALIFORNIA STATE UNIVERSITY, SACRAMENTO. 1976 to 1980

GRAPHIC DESIGNER, University Art Gallery

Emphasis in Art and Psychology.

California State University, Chico. Spring 1983

SAN JOAQUIN DELTA JUNIOR COLLEGE, Stockton, CA. 1974 to 1975

GRAPHIC DESIGNER, Impulse Magazine

Associate of Arts with Honors in Psychology

California State University, Chico. Spring 1982

INTERIOR DESIGNER, John Breuner Furniture Co., Sacramento, CA. 1978 to 1979

Interior Designer Trainee, 1977 to 1978. Sales Clerk, 1976 to 1977

AWARDS AND SCHOLARSHIPS

SCHOLARSHIP AWARD, Book Builders West

San Francisco, CA. 1983

CERTIFICATE OF DISTINCTION, Annual Design Show

California State University, Chico. 1982

FIRST PLACE COVER DESIGN, California State Universities

and Colleges Application Information Booklet

California State University, Chico. 1981

REFERENCES AVAILABLE

Design: Elizabeth Mekjavich
Type: Eras
Ink: Gray, Blue
Paper: White Cambric Cover

94

Daniel N. Frazier

2826 Piedmont Ave.
Berkeley, CA 94705
415.548.6602

EDUCATION

1983
Bachelor of Arts,
Visual Communications
California State University, Chico

Studies: typography, package
design, publication design,
environmental graphics, advertising
design and corporate identity.

ACTIVITIES

1983
Student Design Show
California State University, Chico
Director and Designer.

1981 to 1983
Designers in Progress
California State University, Chico
President.

1981 to 1983
Art Directors and Artists Club
Sacramento, CA

EMPLOYMENT HISTORY

1983
Media Screenprint/Media Design
Chico, CA
Production artist; designer.

1982
Internship
Instructional Media Center
California State University, Chico
Graphic Designer.

1978 to 1981
Bay Alarm Co.
Oakland, CA
Division manager.

1975 to 1977
Krause's Horticultural Service
Reedley, CA
Division manager.

AWARDS

First Award
Chico Fly Fishing Club
Identity Competition

Second Award
Northern California Library
Connection
Vehicle Identity Competition

First Award
Chico Designer Shirt
Competition

References furnished upon request.

Design: Dan Frazier
Type: Helvetica, Garamond
Effects: Blind Emboss
Ink: Gray
Paper: Ivory Cranes Crest, 24 lb.

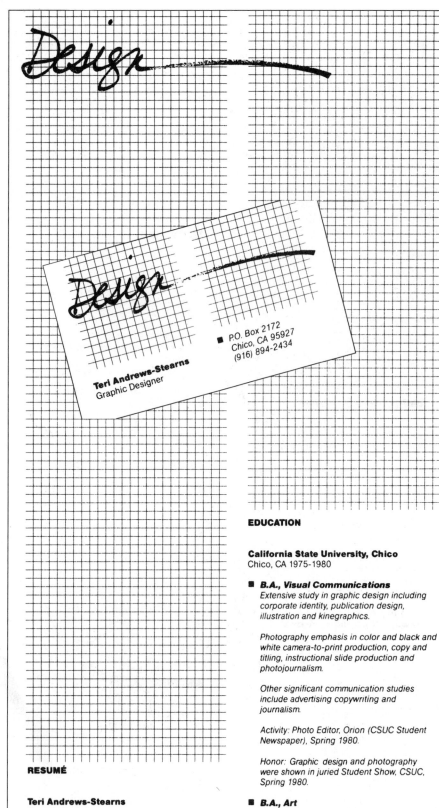

P.O. Box 2172
Chico, CA 95927
(916) 894-2434

Teri Andrews-Stearns
Graphic Designer

EDUCATION

California State University, Chico
Chico, CA 1975-1980

- **B.A., Visual Communications**
  Extensive study in graphic design including corporate identity, publication design, illustration and kinegraphics.

  Photography emphasis in color and black and white camera-to-print production, copy and titling, instructional slide production and photojournalism.

  Other significant communication studies include advertising copywriting and journalism.

  Activity: Photo Editor, Orion (CSUC Student Newspaper), Spring 1980.

  Honor: Graphic design and photography were shown in juried Student Show, CSUC, Spring 1980.

- **B.A., Art**
  Emphasis on multi-media painting, drawing and printmaking.

- **Minor, Business**
  Course work in marketing, management, computerized applications, financial and managerial accounting, business writing and business law.

EXPERIENCE

Andrews-Stearns Design/Photography
Chico, CA   1978 — Present

- *Clients include Pacific Gas and Electric, Butte Savings and Loan Association, Feather River Hospital, and Chico Chamber of Commerce.*

  Other design areas: living/working spaces, costume/garment/textiles and landscaping.

Ray's Liquor
Chico, CA   1981 — Present

- *Graphic design for brochures, advertisements, photography, posters, billboards and flyers.*

Student Assistant, Student Affairs Office
California State University, Chico
Chico, CA   Fall 1980

- *Graphic and promotional work for student activities at CSUC.*

Intern, Community Relations Office
Feather River Hospital
Paradise, CA   Fall 1980

- *Graphic design for identity systems, forms, posters, invitations, brochures, photography, slide show production and exhibit design.*

RESUMÉ

Teri Andrews-Stearns
Graphic Designer

- *P.O. Box 2172*
  Chico, CA 95927
  (916) 894-2434

- *References available on request.*

Design: Teri Andrews-Stearns
Type: Helvetica
Ink: Gray, Brick w/thermography
Paper: White Strathmore Cover

Laura Welty

5446 11th Avenue
Sacramento, CA 95820
Phone: (916) 452-2769

Permanent Address
2019 Harris Street
Eureka, CA 95501

Experience

Graphic Design Internship
Instructional Media Center
  CSU/Chico— 1981

Responsibilities included concept
development, client consultation,
preparation of camera ready art,
use of Compugraphic headliner
and vertical Stat camera.

Wine Steward, cocktail waitress
Old Town Bar and Grill and
Volpi's Dinner House
Eureka, CA— 1979-80

Sign Painter
Lemos Construction
Eureka, CA— 1978

Horse Mountain Ski Area
Dr. Jack Walsh, owner

Awards and Shows

Student symbol competition CSU/
  Chico— 1981
Graduated with Honors— 1981
Bank of America Fine Arts
  Award— 1976

Etchings at Fischer Gallery,
  Chico— 1981
Student Watercolor Show
  CSU/Chico— 1981
Red Barn Gallery, Eureka— 1981

Education

B.A. Art and Visual Communication
California State University,
  Chico— 1981
Humboldt State University,
  Arcata— 1976-1979

Corporate Identification
Typography
Rapid Visualization
Publication Design

Figure, Head and Portrait Drawing
Etching, Lithography
Painting
Gallery Production
Aesthetics

Memberships

Art Directors and Artists Club of
  Sacramento
Designers in Progress, Chico

References available upon request.

Design: Laura Welty
Type: Eras
Ink: Black, Magenta
Paper: White Mesa, 60 lb.

Loustau

MARK LOUSTAU
553 Staples Ave.
San Francisco, CA
(415) 587-4514

OBJECTIVE

Position of responsibliity in a creative environment with opportunity for growth as a graphic designer.

EXPERIENCE

Production Artist, ARTWORKS, July 1982 to present. Preparation of camera ready art, use of typositor, stat camera, logo design, development of packaging/ brochure/ annual report comps for client approval.

Design Intern, ARTWORKS, summer 1981. Packaging Design, comp preparation, client consultation.

Graphic Designer, Instructional Media Center, California State University Chico. Poster Design, Lettering, use of Compugraphic Headliner, stat camera, type specing.

Advertising Designer, The Orion, California State University Chico. Retail advertising design and production.

Production Artist, Chico News & Review, Advertising layout and composition, paste up, use of stat camera.

EDUCATION

Bachelor of Arts, Visual Communications, California State University Chico, 1982.

Courses of instruction include: Graphic Arts Principles, Lettering, Typography, Advertising Design, Packaging Design, Television Graphics, Corporate Identity, 35mm Photography, Copy Camera Techniques, Marketing Principles in Advertising.

ACTIVITIES

New York Young Designers Competition, Packaging Category.

American Institute of Architects Northern California Urban Design Competition.

California State University Chico, Department of Marketing Advertising Campaign Seminar.

Member, Designers in Progress, California State University Chico.

Member, San Francisco Advertising Club 2.

Member, Artists in Print, San Francisco.

REFERENCES

Portfolio review and references available upon request.

Design: Mark Loustau
Type: Helvetica
Ink: Red, Black, Gray
Paper: White Shasta, 70 lb.

T A M O Z E L L E

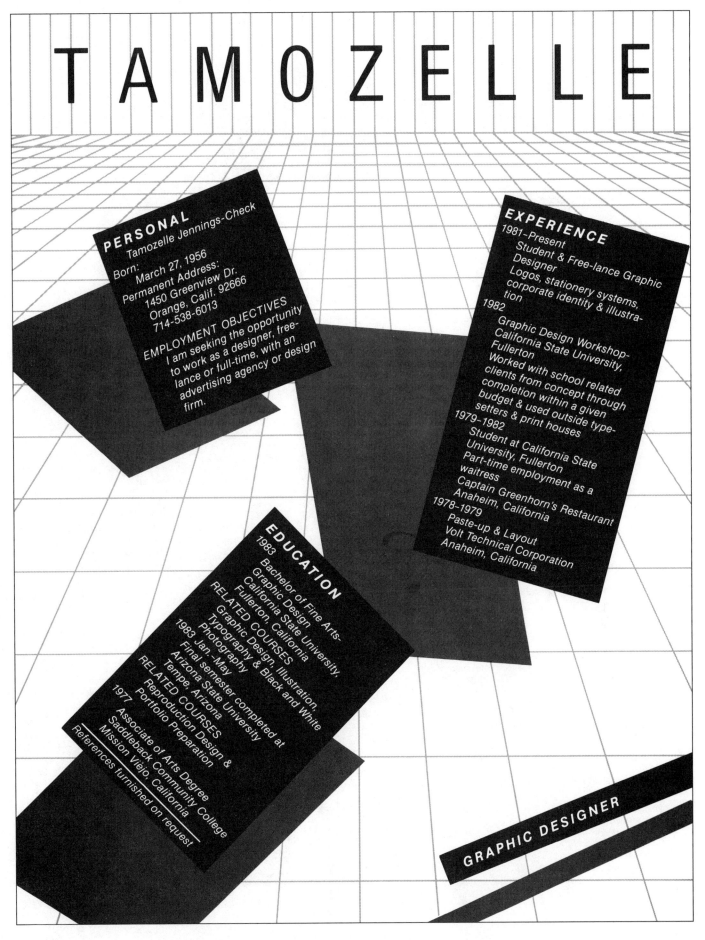

PERSONAL

Tamozelle Jennings-Check

Born:
March 27, 1956
Permanent Address:
1450 Greenview Dr.
Orange, Calif. 92666
714-538-6013

EMPLOYMENT OBJECTIVES
I am seeking the opportunity
to work as a designer, freelance or full-time, with an
advertising agency or design
firm.

EXPERIENCE

1981–Present
Student & Free-lance Graphic
Designer
Logos, stationery systems,
corporate identity & illustra-
tion
1982
Graphic Design Workshop-
California State University,
Fullerton
Worked with school related
clients from concept through
completion within a given
budget & used outside type-
setters & print houses
1979–1982
Student at California State
University, Fullerton
Part-time employment as a
waitress
Captain Greenhorn's Restaurant
Anaheim, California
1978–1979
Paste-up & Layout
Volt Technical Corporation
Anaheim, California

EDUCATION

1983
Bachelor of Fine Arts-
Graphic Design
California State University,
Fullerton, California
RELATED COURSES
Graphic Design, Illustration,
Typography
Photography & Black and White
1983 Jan.–May
Final semester completed at
Arizona State University
Tempe, Arizona
RELATED COURSES
Reproduction Design
Portfolio Preparation
1977
Associate of Arts Degree
Saddleback Community College
Mission Viejo, California
References furnished on request

GRAPHIC DESIGNER

Design: Tamozelle Jennings-Check
Type: Helvetica
Ink: Maroon
Paper: White Kromekote Text

DIANNA DONNER

EXPERIENCE

Graphic Designer–Internship at Instructional Media Center, California State University, Chico.
1981

Responsibilities: Concept Development, client consultation, camera ready art, use of Compugraphic Headliner and stat camera.

Assistant Art Director–**The University Journal** California State University, Chico
1981

Responsibilities: Theme format, type and mechanical specifications, camera ready art.

Production Artist–Creative Concepts Advertising Agency, Riverside, CA
1980

Responsibilities: Preparation of highly finished comps for client approval, camera ready art, mechanical line drawings, and operation of stat camera.

Illustrator–**Inland Empire** Magazine, Riverside, CA
1980

Responsibilities: Design and illustration for editorial and advertising layouts.

Production Assistant–Fleetwood Enterprises, Inc., Printing Division, Riverside, CA
1979

Responsibilities: Collation and bindery.

MEMBERSHIPS

Art Directors and Artists Club of Sacramento
Designers in Progress, CSUC

References upon request.

EDUCATION

Bachelor of Arts, California State University, Chico Visual Communications, 1981.
Emphasis in: Corporate Identity, Kinegraphics, Publication Design, Typography, and Photography.

University of North Alabama, Florence, Alabama
1977-1979
Completed general education, with an emphasis in studio art.

5479 Argyle Way
Riverside, CA 92506
(714) 686-1382

Design: Dianna Donner-Zapata
Type: Avant Garde
Effects: Die Cut
Ink: Blue, Magenta
Paper: White Karma Cover

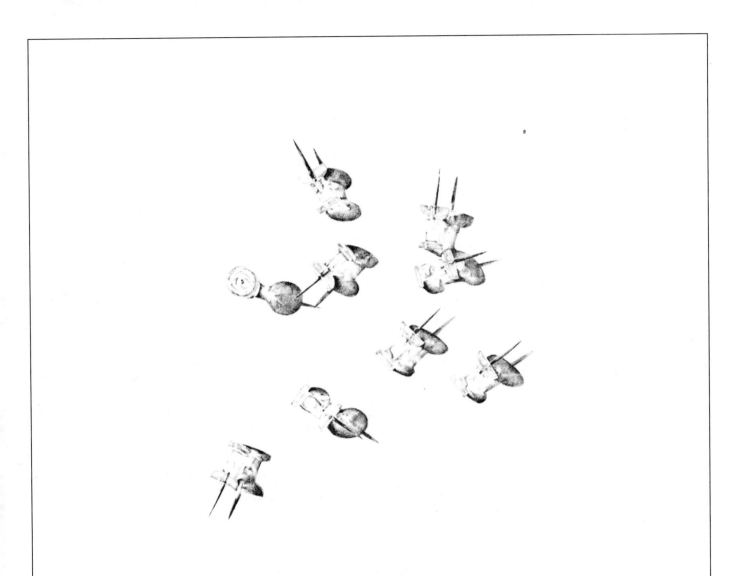

Craig B. Frazier
22 years of age
Excellent health
408 Ivy St. #6   (916) 345-3934
Chico, CA 95926
Alternate address
670 Vernon St. #203   (415) 428-1930
Oakland, CA 94610

Education
Bachelor of Arts, CSU Chico, 8/1/78
Visual Communications, G.P.A. 3.68
Emphasis of study
Art
Corporate identity
Creative problem solving
Environmental design
Illustration
Magazine production
Packaging
Photography
Television graphics
Typography

Experience
Internship, Campus graphics
CSU Chico, 9/1/77 - 12/20/77
Freelance illustration, Image Group
Chico, 12/1/77 - present

Memberships/Distinctions
Member of ADAC, Sacramento
Honor Award
Envision 4 student show
Three Honor Awards
CSUC student show 1978
References furnished upon request

Design: Craig Frazier
Illustration: Craig Frazier
Type: Palatino
Ink: Black
Paper: White Karma Text, 80 lb.

Experience
Chico News & Review
Editorial Design
April 1982 to June 1983
Principal staff design position.
Responsibilities include design,
production & organization of editorial
content for a weekly newsmagazine,
circulation 29,000. Art directed
current mastbead, contributed
photography & helped coordinate
promotional materials.
Staff Designer
September 1981 to April 1982
Designed advertising & editorial
layouts, in-house promotions.

Gene Clark Design & Lettering
April 1980 to Present
Freelance design studio, projects
including identities, posters,
publications, advertising &
environmental design, plus
calligraphy, lettering & photography.
Clients include Gwen Amos Design
(Sacramento), D. Randy & Associates
(Laguna Beach), Image Group (Chico),
California State University, Chico,
& a variety of local businesses.

Sundance Records
April 1976 to July 1981
Management position, responsibilities
include all in-store signage & displays,
window displays, sales & purchasing.

Education
California State University, Chico
1975 to 1977, 1980 to 1982
Courses include visual communication,
lettering, typography, publication,
design workshop & photography.

Awards
PG&E Energy Conservation Poster
Competition, 1981
Second place

Shows
CSUC Graphic Design/Photography Show
1981 & 1982
A juried exhibit of student work

Memberships
Designers in Progress
1981 to 1982
Served as vice-president

References available
upon request.

G e n e   C l a r k

R E S U M E

Design: Gene Clark
Type: Helvetica, Garamond
Ink: Gray, Salmon, Light Green
Paper: White Moistrite Matte, 60 lb.

102

Alix Smith
165 Kenwood Way
San Francisco, Ca
94127
415.589.2993

EXPERIENCE	**Designer** Graphic Works Chico, Ca	July 1982 through June 1983 Clients included Pacific Express, Caribou Mountaineering, West Air. Serviced accounts from concept through production. Tracked expenses, contracted freelancers, operated horizontal process camera and AM Varityper computerized typesetting equipment.
	Production Manager Chico News & Review Chico, Ca	April 1982 through June 1982 Supervised staff of six designers in the production of weekly newspaper, circulation 29,000. Coordinated typesetting and camera schedules, ordered supplies.
	Staff Designer Chico News & Review Chico, Ca	July 1980 through March 1982 Designed and produced editorial and advertising layouts on a weekly basis. Created ad campaigns and produced promotional materials for sales staff. One year as elected staff representative to management committee.
	Design Intern Chico News & Review Chico, Ca	June 1979 through December 1979 Designed and produced weekly pull-out calendar of events. Composed radio spots.
	Designer & Photographer Dog Day Design Chico, Ca	September 1978 to present Freelanced for a variety of clients including a radio station, a theatre troupe and clothing stores. Produced logos, advertising campaigns, posters and announcements.
	Photographer University of Maine Fort Kent, Me	September 1976 through May 1977 Supplied black & white and color photographs for press releases, catalogs and university system promotionals.
EDUCATION	Experimental Typography California State University Chico, Ca	September 1982 to December 1982
	Bachelor of Arts California State University Chico, Ca	Degree awarded May 1980 Visual Communication Major Photography/Industrial Technology Minor
	California State College Bakersfield, Ca	January 1975 to June 1976 January 1978 to June 1978 Photography and Biology concentration
	University of Maine Fort Kent, Me	August 1976 to May 1977 Genetics concentration
AWARDS & SHOWS	1st Place CSB Alumni Association Logo Competition	January 1979
	2nd Place PG&E Energy Conservation Logo Competition	April 1980
	Photography Honor Award Design Honor Award CSUC Annual Juried Student Show	May 1979 & May 1980 May 1979
PERSONAL	Born 7-31-56	Single and healthy
	Professional affiliations	ADAC 1979 to present DIP's 1979 to 1980
	Interests	Biological Trivia, Photography, Dogs
	References	Available upon request

Design: Alix Smith
Type: Helvetica Condensed
Ink: Gray, Lilac
Paper: White Karma Cover

SUZANNE GUTTMAN

124 Los Cerros, Walnut Creek, CA 94598   (415) 944-9139

Education

1981
BA Visual Communication California State University, Chico Studies include; graphic design, advertising and photography.

1979-80
University of Massachusetts. Amherst, Massachusetts. National Student Exchange, studied Marketing and business

1977-78
American River College Sacramento, California Liberal Studies

1977
Marconi Technical School Sacramento, California High school vocational program. Studied an overview of commercial art skills.

Work Experience

1981
Feather River Hospital, Paradise, CA Community Relations Department Internship. Graphic Designer; responsible for publication, ad design, and copywriting.

1981
Instructionally Related Activities CSUC, Chico, CA Graphic Designer; responsible for ad design for weekly sports newspaper, publication design and client consultation.

1980
Massachusetts Daily Collegian Amherst, Mass. University Daily newspaper. Responsible for layout design and paste-up.

1977
ComCo- Communications Company Sacramento, CA Responsible for paste-up, layout, copy camera, ad design.

Memberships

1979-81
Designers in Progress CSUC

1977-81
Art Directors and Artist Club of Sacramento Sacramento, CA. Attended Envisions 5 & 7.

1980-81
Sacramento Women in Advertising Sacramento, CA

1980
Marketing Club, CSUC.

Awards

1981
Young Designers Competition Packaging Category Participation award of Merit.

1980
Advertising Seminar Cal. State, Chico Group Coordinator, Second place.

REFERENCES AVAILABLE UPON REQUEST.

Design: Suzanne Guttman
Type: Frutiger
Ink: Dark Blue, Magenta
Paper: Gray Gilbert Linen, 24 lb.

Objectives:

If you're looking for a contemporary designer who stands out in a crowd, who sticks her neck out to create new, exciting solutions to the problems of visual communication, look no further.... I fit the bill.

Education:

1980-1981	Arizona State University
1977-1979	Tempe, Arizona
	BFA in Graphic Design
	Emphasis: Business
	and Industrial
	Publication Design,
	Corporate Identity
	Programs, Logo Design,
	Environmental Graphics,
	Illustration, Photography,
	Serigraphy, Color Theory,
	Graphic Arts Techniques
	and Darkroom Processes
1976	Instituto Allende
	San Miguel Allende
	Guanajuato, Mexico
	Emphasis: Life Drawing,
	Painting, Spanish
1975-1976	Pima Community College
	Tucson, Arizona
	Emphasis: Business
1974-1975	University of Arizona
	Tucson, Arizona
	Emphasis: Drawing
1974	Central Arizona College
	Coolidge, Arizona
	Emphasis: Portrait Painting

Employment:

1977-	Freelance Design
	Phoenix and Los Angeles
	Jobs in Graphic Design,
	Magazine Layout and
	Design, Illustration,
	Serigraphy, and Painting
1977-	Bartender
	Jolly Roger Restaurant
	Tempe, Arizona
1979	Cabin Attendant
	Delta Queen Steamboat
	New Orleans, Louisiana

Activities:

1977-	Scottsdale Artists League
	Membership
1980-1981	Graphicus Club Membership
	(ASU Graphic Design
	Organization)
1977-1981	Dean's List (ASU)
1975-1976	Dean's List (PCC)
1974-1975	Tuition Scholarship (UA)
1970-1974	National Honor Society
1970-1972	California Scholarship
	Federation
1978-	Serigraphs and Paintings
	exhibited in
	Camelview Plaza Gallery
	Scottsdale, Arizona
1979-1980	Serigraphs exhibited in
	Scottsdale Memorial
	Hospital
	Scottsdale, Arizona
1979	Poster exhibited in ASU
	Graphic Design Show
1977	Photograph exhibited in
	ASU Self-Portrait
	Photography Show

Personal:

P.O. Box 27032
Tempe, Arizona 85282
(602) 897-0607

Born September 6, 1957
Long Beach, California
Single, Excellent Health
Interests: Travel, Dance, Music,
Photography, Printmaking, Snow and
Water Sports

References available upon request

Design: Karin Burklein
Illustration: Karin Burklein
Type: Avant Garde
Ink: Dark Blue, Pink
Paper: White Centura Text, 80 lb.

R E S U M E

Thomas J. Saputo
38 Sandra Court
Newbury Park, CA 91320
805•498•3229

Education:

Bachelor of Arts
Visual Communications
California State University,
Chico, Spring 1980
Studies included: corporate
identity, publication design,
packaging, typography,
environmental design,
photography, kinegraphics.

Associate Arts
Liberal Studies
Moorpark College
Spring 1976

Work Experience:

Art Director:
Student Profile of Instructors,
1979-1980
Position included production
cost evaluation, layout and
design. Publication selected for
display in 1980 CICS Student
Design Show.

Advertising sales/design
Chico News & Review
Chico CA, 1978-1979
The position included
responsibility for advertising
design and sales. Initiated,
maintained and billed
accounts, served on
management committees and
produced complete
advertisements. Gained
experience with horizontal
copy camera and
Compugraphic headline
typesetter.

Awards & Exhibits:

1979 Pacific Gas & Electric
Energy Conservation
Logo Competition.
Two cash awards.

1980 CICS Student Show
Three design pieces selected
by professional jury
for exhibition.

Memberships:

Art Directors and Artists' Club
of Sacramento 1979/1980

Designers in Progress
CSU/Chico 1979/1980

References upon request.

Design: Tom Saputo
Type: Palatino
Ink: Brick Red
Paper: Karma Natural Text, 80 lb.

John Chase
25 Corutn Dr.
Alamo, CA 94507
(415) 837-9277

Education

1978 - 1982

BA - Visual Communications
Minor - Art/Industrial Technology
California State University, Chico

Emphasis: Corporate identity,
environmental graphics, computer
graphics, lettering, typography,
advertising design, publication design,
photography, offset lithography.

Experience

1979 - 1981

Graphic designer –
Cherry Street High Fidelity
Chico, CA

Conceptualized and designed newspaper
ads. In-house graphics.

1978 - 1979

Graphic designer –
Community Action Volunteers in
Education
C.S.U., Chico

Did volunteer graphic design work for
annual newspaper, flyers.

Awards

1982

Honor Award
Juried student annual show
"Corporate Symbol"

Cash Award
Kiosk Exhibit
California Library Association

1981

Cash Award
Symbol
Glenn Memorial Hospital

Cash Award
Symbol
Bidwell Golf Club

1979

Honorable Mention
Symbol
PG&E Logo Competition

1976

Prize Award
Illustration
Cartoons Magazine

Workshops/Conferences

1983

San Francisco Advertising Club
Annual design show and awards
banquet

1980 - 82

"Envision"
Annual Western Design Conference
Sacramento, CA

1981

Designer's Roundtable
Slide production workshop and
portfolio show
Portland, OR

Freelance

1983

Conceptualized and designed annual
conference folder, program, t-shirts and
registration forms for CSU Chico Housing
Office.

Designed logo and business system for
Contacht (Mountain View).

1982

Designed logos, business systems, and
promotional art for Creative
Environments (Alamo, CA), Crystal
Cosmetics (Danville, CA), and the City
of Los Gatos Recycling Program
(Los Gatos, CA).

References available on request.

Design: John Chase
Type: Benguiat
Ink: Red, Gray
Paper: White Karma Text, 80 lb.

GRAPHICS

SALLY COHN
2150 Oakley Ave.
Menlo Park, CA 94025
415.854.3397

Born 3.23.60

EDUCATION
1983
BA in Visual Communication
California State University, Chico

Major Emphasis
Publication Design, corporate identity, typography,
advertising design, lettering, package design,
environmental graphics, kinegraphics, calligraphy, and
photography

Minor Emphasis
advertising, marketing, management, accounting, and
economics

INTERNSHIPS / WORK EXPERIENCE
1983
Graphic Designer
Instructional Media Center
California State University, Chico

Responsibilities included concept development, client
consultation, preparation of camera-ready art,
operation of compugraphic headliner and vertical stat
camera

1981-1983
Childcare
Kangaroo Kourts
Chico, CA

Responsibilities included supervising children, toddlers
and infants

1981
Customer Service
The Kopy Kid
Chico, CA

Responsibilites included cashier, copy machines, spiral
binding, velo-binding

1979
Photographic Printer
Drewry Photocolor Co.
San Carlos, CA

Responsibilities included handling negatives for fast
photo print machine

CONFERENCE
1983
Envision Nine
Sacramento, CA

EXHIBIT
1983 Annual Student Show
Juried Graphic Design Exhibit
California State University, Chico

CLUBS
1983
Art Directors and Artists Club
Sacramento, CA

Designers in Progress
Chico, CA

A list of personal references is available upon your
request

Design: Sally Cohn
Type: Avant Garde, Lubalin Graph
Ink: Wine, Silver Varnish
Paper: White Karma Text, 100 lb.

GRADUATE

1982
B.A. in Visual Communication
California State University, Chico

Emphasis
Publication design, corporate identity,
advertising design, typography, lettering, and
environmental graphics.

REFERENCES

Available upon request.

ACTIVITIES

1980, 82
Envision 6 and 8
Sacramento, CA
1981
Business of Design Conference
Sacramento, CA

PERSONAL

Kathryn Sturges
6058 Calle de Rico
San Jose, CA 95124
408.267.1415

Born: 11.6.59
Married
Excellent health.

HONORS/AWARDS

1982-83
Outstanding Visual Communicator Award
1982
Honors in Exhibit Competition
North State Co-operative Library System
1982
Award of Merit
Young Designer's Packaging Competition
1982
Certificates of Distinction:
Best in Environmental Graphics
Best in Packaging
CSUC Student Graphic Show

INTERNSHIPS/EXPERIENCE

1982-83
Sturges Design
Self Employment
1982
Graphic Designer
Instructional Media Center
CSU Chico
Responsibilities included:
concept development, client consultation,
preparation of camera-ready art, use of
Compugraphic headliner, and stat camera.
1982
Graphic Designer
The Smith Bros. Marketing and Graphic
Design
Sacramento
Responsibilities included:
concept development, client consultation, and
preparation of camera-ready art.
1981
Graphic Designer
Gwen Amos Design
Sacramento
Responsibilities included:
illustration, concept development, and
preparation of camera-ready art.

CLUBS

ADAC, Sacramento

Design: Kathryn Sturges
Type: Helvetica
Ink: Gray, Magenta-Blue Split Fountain
Paper: White Karma Text, 100 lb.

Rose Hodges
454 E 8th Street #2
Chico. CA 95926

Photography

Resume

Work Experience

Education

Activities

1980-81
Freelance Photographer — responsible for major drama productions at CSU. Chico. support photography for weekly newspaper. Chico News and Review and University newspaper. The Orion: portrait work: advertising photography

1979-81
California State University. Chico: studies in Visual Communications with an emphasis in Graphic Design and Photography

Art Directors and Artists Club. Sacramento
Designers In Progress. Chico

1980
Lab Technician —
La Force Color Lab. Chico

Courses included: Studio Lighting. Product and Advertising Photography. Color Photography. Copying and Titling. Visual Concepts. Photo-mechanical Reproduction. Lettering. Typography. Publication Design and Package Design

Exhibitions

1979-80
Photojournalist —
CSU. Chico. Record Yearbook

1977
Bachelor of Arts Degree in Recreation Administration
California State University. Chico

Chico Creative Arts
Learning Resource Center. CSU. Chico
Student Competition in Communications CSU.. Chico

Workshops

Travel — Europe '80 Designers tour London, Basel. Paris. Extensive travel in Europe and residency in London and Frankfurt.

Light Language   1981   Sacramento
Charles Kemper   1980   Sacramento
Penina Meisel   1980   Sacramento
Nikon Weekend   1979   San Francisco
Canon   1979   South Lake Tahoe

Design: Rose Hodges
Type: Helvetica
Ink: Green, Rose
Paper: Karma Natural Cover

education

1983
Bachelor of Art
Visual Communications;
emphasis in photography
California State University, Chico

Course of Study
Studio lighting/Bank lighting,
Advertising/Product photography,
Portrait photography,
Photojournalism, News and
copywriting, Screenprinting,
and Marketing skills.

memberships

Women in Communications,
Chico Ca.
Designers in Progress, Chico Ca.
Communications Club, Chico Ca.
Marketing Club, Chico Ca.

exhibits

1980
CSU Chico Meriam Library.
1979
Fisher Gallery, Chico Ca.
Community display, Chico Ca.
Butte College Campus Center,
Chico Ca.

experience

1982-1983
Instructional Media Center
CSU Chico
Photographer
Responsibilities include: Working
directly with designers to fulfill
their photographic needs. Use of
high speed film with available light
to photograph dramatic events.
Photographed and
printed for University catalog.
Using annual report format in
developing brochures for
University departments. Standard
processing of film and running
machine process of E6.
1982-1983
Freelance Photographer
Responsibilities include:
Advertising photography, passport
and portrait photography.
1980-1982
Meriam Library
CSU Chico
Student Assistant
Responsibilities include: Working
with the public. Operation and
maintenance of non-print
equipment. Use of keyboard
computers, and clerical work.
1979-1980
Photojournalist
CSU Chico Record Yearbook

special projects

1982
Developed a complete slide/tape
presentation on the social and
psychological effects of Graffiti.

In a group situation developed a
major marketing proposal for
P.G.E. using multi-media.
1981
Designed and photographed
publicity campaign for
Phi Kappa Tau fraternity's
sheriff candidate.

Wrote, directed and, produced
a 10 minute
documentary film
on the world of the deaf;
''A World of Silence.''

Researched and wrote
an extensive paper on Subliminal
Advertising, including visual aids.

workshops

1982
Slide Presentation workshop,
Chico Ca.
Color and Pigments, Chico Ca.
1981
Studio Bank Lighting, Chico Ca.
1979
Photo Field Experience, Chico Ca.
Nikon Weekend, San Francisco Ca.
1977
Photo and Sound Company,
San Francisco Ca.

personal

Julie Schroer
276 East 7th Avenue
Chico, Ca 95926
(916) 342.2127
(916) 891.6534

Portfolio and References available
on request.

Design: Kathryn Sturges
Photography: Cec Green
Type: Helvetica
Ink: Black
Paper: White Flokote, 70 lb.

Leslie Flores

Leslie Flores
935 Bryant Ave.
Chico, CA 95926
916 342 0217

Education

1981
B.A. in Visual Communications
California State University, Chico

1977
Certificate of Completion
The Glen Fishback School
of Photography

Job Objective

Position as documentary
photographer for publications.

Experience

1982
Pin One On
Photo Pin Business
Co-owner

1977-Present
Freelance Photographer
Chico News & Review

1979-1981
Staff Photographer
Instructional Media Center
CSUC

1977-1978
Photographer
Impulse Magazines
Orion, Student Newspaper
CSUC

Awards

1981, 1979, 1977
Best in Show
1980, 1978
First Place
Silver Dollar Fair, Chico

1980
Honor Award
University/College Designers
Association

1978-1981
7 Honor Awards
CSUC Student Show

Exhibits

1982
Retrospective
LaSalles Restaurant, Chico

1981, 1978
Learning Center, CSUC

1980
Creative Arts Center, Chico

1977
Women's Center, Chico

Workshops

1982
Tahoe Photographic Workshop
Documentary
Mary Ellen Mark

1982
Maple House Photography Lectures
Fremont, CA

1981
The Friends of Photography
Members Workshop
Carmel, CA

Memberships

The Friends of Photography, Carmel
Sacramento Art Directors Club
Designers in Progress, Chico

References upon request

Design: Mark Ulriksen
Photographer: Leslie Flores
Type: Helvetica
Ink: Black and Sienna Duatone
Paper: White Shasta Suede Cover

Self-Portrait
1982

Laguna Beach Ladies
1981

AWARDS

1981
Outstanding Visual Communicator Award
California State University, Chico

1981
Honorable Mention
Camera Portfolio Magazine

1979, 1980, 1981
Best in Show, Photography
CSU-Chico Student
Visual Communication Annual

1979, 1980, 1981
5 Honor Awards
CSU-Chico Student
Visual Communication Annual

1980
Best in Show, Photography
Silver Dollar Regional Fair
Chico, CA

EXHIBITIONS

1982
La Salles Restaurant
Chico, CA

1982
Bell Camera, Inc.
Chico, CA

1981
Omni Arts Show
Chico, CA

1978, 1981
Meriam Library, CSU-Chico
Chico, CA

1980
Creative Arts Center
Chico, CA

1977
Women's Center Gallery
Chico, CA

1977
Bell Memorial Union, CSU-Chico
Chico, CA

WORKSHOPS/CONFERENCES

1982
Tahoe Photographic Workshop
Documentary
Mary Ellen Mark

1978, 1979, 1980, 1981, 1982
Envision/Design Conferences
Sacramento, CA

1982
Maple House Photography Lectures
Fremont, CA

1981
The Friends of Photography
Members' Workshop
Carmel, CA

1975
Aperture '75/Photography Conference
Chico, CA

References upon request

Pool Chairs
1979

Legs
1982

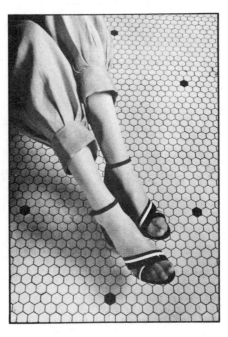

EDUCATION

1981
Bachelor of Arts Degree
Visual Communications
California State University, Chico

1977
Certificate of Achievement
The Glen Fishback School
of Photography
Sacramento, CA

EXPERIENCE

1978-1982
Staff Photographer
University Relations/Alumni Office
California State University, Chico

Responsibilities included photography
for alumni newspaper, annual reports,
university catalogs, brochures, and
publicity releases.

1977-present
Freelance Photographer
Publication, documentary,
portrait, brochure, catalog,
and advertising photography.
Multimedia slide presentations.

1982-present
Pin One On
Photo Pin Business
Co-Owner

1977-1978
Photographer
Activities Office
California State University, Chico

Responsibilities included publicity
photographs for sporting events,
drama productions, and art
exhibitions.

1978, 1981, 1982
Photographer
Impulse Magazine
California State University, Chico

MEMBERSHIPS

Art Directors and Artists Club
Sacramento, CA

The Friends of Photography
Carmel, CA

Women in Communications, Inc.
National Chapter
Chico Chapter

Designers in Progress
Chico, CA

Design: Mark Ulriksen
Photography: Monica Lee
Type: Palatino
Ink: Black
Paper: White Shasta Suede Cover

113

WAIF MULLINS

370 East Lassen Avenue
Space 41
Chico, CA 95926
916/343-8401

EDUCATION

1972
California State University, Chico
Bachelor of Arts (Painting Emphasis)

1980
California State University, Chico
Master of Arts (Painting Emphasis)

AWARDS

"Since childhood, my main goal has been to make a living from my art."

Waif began painting at age 11. Since then his work has won over 40 awards in juried shows, including:

1971
Third Annual Yuba College Open
Best of Show

1972
Sacramento Festival of the Arts
Two Purchase Awards

Northern California Arts
Membership Show
One of five Merit Awards
One of ten Honorable Mentions

1973
Winnie A. Porter, juried art show
Best of Show

PUBLISHED ARTWORK

"My work is always created with an emphasis on compositional elements which are very similar to music, composed with harmonies, dissidents, texture… to create mood and feeling."

Waif's published artwork is included in:
A Practical Guide for Beginning Painters
By Tom Griffith
Prentice Hall, Inc., publishers
Nature Drawing: a tool for learning.
By Claire Walker Leslie
Prentice Hall, Inc., publishers
Phantasm Magazine
Featured Artist
Heidelberg Graphics, publishers

ART SHOWS

"I enjoy working in all mediums from sculpture to pastel."

Currently, he is directing his energy toward developing his distinctive print media. His works have been displayed in 10 one-man shows, 4 two-man shows, and in such galleries as:

Arts and Crafts Gallery, Chico, CA
Fischer Gallery, Chico, CA
Galerie, San Francisco, CA
Village Gallery, Sacramento, CA
Yellowstone Art Center, Billings, MT

PUBLIC COLLECTIONS

"I prefer to work on location, rather than from photos, because I can view my subjects from all angles before starting. I also avoid photos because I don't feel they give a full and accurate color range."

Works in public collections include:
Famous Artists Schools
Traveling Collection
California State University, Chico
Permanent Collection
Yuba College
Permanent Collection

RESUMÉ

Design: Linda Clark Johnson
Type: Palatino
Ink: Black
Paper: White Quintessence, 80 lb.

Steve Tackett-Barbaria
389 E. 7th St. Chico CA 95926
(916) 891-0530

Professional Experience
Illustrator/designer, Chico News & Review
Illustrations from concept to completion in pencil,
pen and ink, air brush, and ink wash on a limitless
number of subjects; Weekly political cartoon titled
The Satirical Line; Manager of Graphic Works, a
separate design business within the Chico News &
Review; Extensive use of stat camera and
compugraphic headliner.
1978-present

Illustrator/Designer
Community Action Volunteers In
Education (C.A.V.E.)
Illustrator for news magazine; production of
promotional material.
1977-1978

Education
Canada College
Redwood City CA
Emphasis: Drawing, painting, and
printmaking
1975-1977

California State University at Chico
Emphasis: Drawing, painting,
printmaking, graphic design, and
publication production
Bachelor of Arts
Fine Arts fall 1978

Exhibitions
Canada College
Group student show
1976

CSUC
Illustration and Design show
1979

Wall Mural
Patio of Madison Bear Gardens
Chico CA
Completed by a group of 7 artists
38'x188'—1978

Wall Mural
CSUC Campus
Individual work
10'x15'—1979

Awards
Grand Award
Illustration for print media
Sacramento Women In Advertising
1978

''Square Within a Square''
Painting chosen for permanent
collection
Canada College
8'x10' 1977

Memberships/conferences
''Envision'' design conference
1978 and 1979

Art Directors and Artists Club
Sacramento CA
1979-present

115

Design: Steve Tackett-Barbaria
Illustration: Steve Tackett-Barbaria
Type: Helvetica
Ink: Black
Paper: Skytone Natural Vellum Cover

PROGRAM CHART IS ON A-26

Saturday

8 PM ❸ ART TO ART

While attending an international designer show, Jennifer (Stefanie Powers) overhears a plot to steal many valuable pieces of art. Jonathan: Robert Wagner. (Repeat; 60 min.)

❺ THE MAN FROM U&LC

Solo disguishes himself as a THRUST agent in order to save the Helvetica family from being completely eliminated. Solo: Robert Vaughn. Kuryakin: David McCallum. (60 min.)

❽ RESUME–Profile

Details of "Harry Chang: A Designer with a Difference" are in the Close-up.

⓬ HILL STREET HUES

Furillo (Daniel J. Travanti) becomes involved in a deep discussion with the art director over the origins of the color green; LaRue (Kiel Martin) celebrates when the art director gives him permission to paint his studio pink; Belker (Bruce Weitz) stakes out

an art supply store for Dr. Martin dyes. (Repeat; 60 min.)

⓾ MAGNUM, A.D.

Magnum (Tom Selleck) has a tough decision between the PLAYBOY account or the account of a retirement community worth twice as much. Higgins: John Hillerman. (60 min.)

9 PM ❸ T-SQUARE HOOKER

Hooker (William Shatner) goes on a long trek to find the proper t-square that will fit his drawing board. Romano: Adrian Zmed. (60 min.)

⓬ FRAME·

As the students prepare for the annual art show, the frame shop burns down, forcing them to frame their own work. Lydia: Debbie Allen. Danny: Carlo Imperto. (60 min.)

⓾ DYES OF HAZZARD

When Hogg sells a worthless piece of art to a newlywed couple, the Dyes turn the tables on him with a few

---

**RESUME
8 PM ❽**

**HARRY CHANG:
A DESIGNER WITH A DIFFERENCE**

This week's resume is a profile featuring Harry Chang, who is actively seeking an opportunity for a career position in the graphic design field.

EDUCATION

1983 Bachelor of Fine Arts Degree in Graphic Design, Arizona State University, Tempe, Arizona.

1979 Associated Arts Degree in Liberal Arts, Glendale Community College, Glendale, Arizona.

EXPERIENCE

1982 In class freelance design- KQYT calendar, selected third.

1981 In class freelance design- PHOENIX CASTING NEWS, a departmental masthead, selected first.

1977- Moon Valley Market, Phoenix, Arizona, a part-time job in inventory, stocking and check-out.

AWARDS

1979 Phi Theta Kappa Honor Society.

PERSONAL

Harry Chang
1926 West Cactus Road
Phoenix, Arizona 85029
(602) 943-0239

References available upon request.

Design: Harry Chang
Type: IBM Univers
Ink: Black
Paper: Gray Bond, 20 lb.

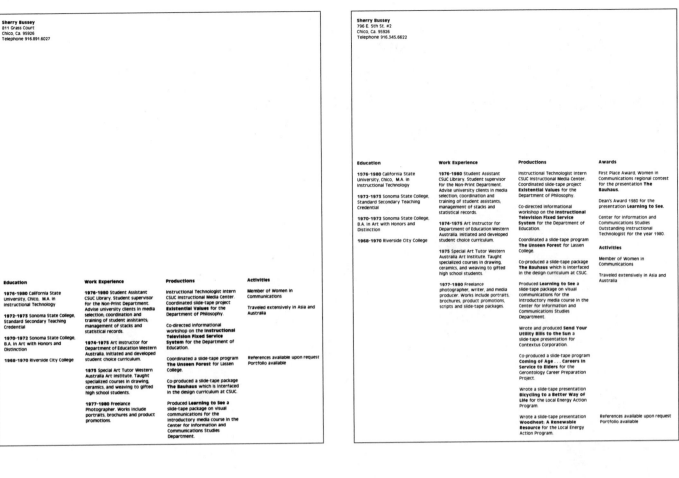

Sherry Bussey
811 Grass Court
Chico, Ca. 95926
Telephone 916.891.6027

Education

1976-1980 California State University, Chico, M.A. in Instructional Technology

1972-1975 Sonoma State College, Standard Secondary Teaching Credential

1970-1972 Sonoma State College, B.A. in Art with Honors and Distinction

1968-1970 Riverside City College

Work Experience

1976-1980 Student Assistant CSUC Library. Student supervisor for the Non-Print Department. Advise university clients in media selection; coordination and training of student assistants; management of stacks and statistical records.

1974-1975 Art instructor for Department of Education Western Australia. Initiated and developed student choice curriculum.

1975 Special Art Tutor Western Australia Art Institute. Taught specialized courses in drawing, ceramics, and weaving to gifted high school students.

1977-1980 Freelance Photographer. Works include portraits, brochures and product promotions.

Productions

Instructional Technologist intern CSUC Instructional Media Center. Coordinated slide-tape project **Existential Values** for the Department of Philosophy.

Co-directed informational workshop on the **Instructional Television Fixed Service System** for the Department of Education.

Coordinated a slide-tape program **The Unseen Forest** for Lassen College.

Co-produced a slide-tape package **The Bauhaus** which is interfaced in the design curriculum at CSUC.

Produced **Learning to See** a slide-tape package on visual communications for the introductory media course in the Center for Information and Communications Studies Department.

Activities

Member of Women in Communications

Traveled extensively in Asia and Australia

References available upon request
Portfolio available

Sherry Bussey
796 E. 5th St. #2
Chico, Ca. 95926
Telephone 916.345.6622

Education

1976-1980 California State University, Chico, M.A. in Instructional Technology

1972-1975 Sonoma State College, Standard Secondary Teaching Credential

1970-1972 Sonoma State College, B.A. in Art with Honors and Distinction

1968-1970 Riverside City College

Work Experience

1976-1980 Student Assistant CSUC Library. Student supervisor for the Non-Print Department. Advise university clients in media selection; coordination and training of student assistants; management of stacks and statistical records.

1974-1975 Art instructor for Department of Education Western Australia. Initiated and developed student choice curriculum.

1975 Special Art Tutor Western Australia Art Institute. Taught specialized courses in drawing, ceramics, and weaving to gifted high school students.

1977-1980 Freelance photographer, writer, and media producer. Works include portraits, brochures, product promotions, scripts and slide-tape packages.

Productions

Instructional Technologist intern CSUC Instructional Media Center. Coordinated slide-tape project **Existential Values** for the Department of Philosophy.

Co-directed informational workshop on the **Instructional Television Fixed Service System** for the Department of Education.

Coordinated a slide-tape program **The Unseen Forest** for Lassen College.

Co-produced a slide-tape package **The Bauhaus** which is interfaced in the design curriculum at CSUC.

Produced **Learning to See** a slide-tape package on visual communications for the introductory media course in the Center for Information and Communications Studies Department.

Wrote and produced **Send Your Utility Bills to the Sun** a slide-tape presentation for Contextus Corporation.

Co-produced a slide-tape program **Coming of Age . . . Careers in Service to Elders** for the Gerontology Career Preparation Project.

Wrote a slide-tape presentation **Bicycling to a Better Way of Life** for the Local Energy Action Program.

Wrote a slide-tape presentation **Woodheat: A Renewable Resource** for the Local Energy Action Program.

Awards

First Place Award, Women in Communications regional contest for the presentation **The Bauhaus.**

Dean's Award 1980 for the presentation **Learning to See.**

Center for Information and Communications Studies Outstanding Instructional Technologist for the year 1980.

Activities

Member of Women in Communications

Traveled extensively in Asia and Australia

References available upon request
Portfolio available

Sherry Bussey
811 Grass Court
Chico, Ca. 95926
Telephone 916.891.6027

Education

1976-1980 California State University, Chico, M.A. in Instructional Technology

1972-1973 Sonoma State College, Standard Secondary Teaching Credential

1970-1972 Sonoma State College, B.A. in Art with Honors and Distinction

1968-1970 Riverside City College

Work Experience

1980-1981 Supervisor for the Nonprint Department in the Meriam Library at CSU, Chico. Assist library patrons with media selection and use; coordinate work schedules for student assistants; organize and direct training in the use of audio visual equipment; maintain statistical records; coordinate media use with the Instructional Media Center; conduct searches for Nonprint materials.

1977-1981 Freelance photographer, writer, and media producer. Works include portraits, brochures, product promotions, scripts and slide-tape packages.

1976-1980 Student Assistant CSUC Library. Student supervisor for the Non-Print Department. Advise university clients in media selection; coordination and training of student assistants; management of stacks and statistical records.

1974-1975 Art instructor for Department of Education Western Australia. Initiated and developed student choice curriculum.

1975 Special Art Tutor Western Australia Art Institute. Taught specialized courses in drawing, ceramics, and weaving to gifted high school students.

Productions

Instructional Technologist intern CSUC Instructional Media Center. Coordinated slide-tape project **Existential Values** for the Department of Philosophy.

Co-directed informational workshop on the **Instructional Television Fixed Service System** for the Department of Education.

Coordinated a slide-tape program **The Unseen Forest** for Lassen College.

Co-produced a slide-tape package **The Bauhaus** which is interfaced in the design curriculum at CSUC.

Produced **Learning to See** a slide-tape package on visual communications for the introductory media course in the Center for Information and Communications Studies Department.

Wrote and produced **Send Your Utility Bills to the Sun** a slide-tape presentation for Contextus Corporation.

Co-produced a slide-tape program **Coming of Age . . . Careers in Service to Elders** for the Gerontology Career Preparation Project.

Produced **Artists of Chico** a slide-tape program documenting local visual artists for the Chico Creative Arts Center and the California Arts Council.

Wrote the slide-tape presentations **Bicycling to a Better Way of Life** and **Woodheat: A Renewable Resource** for the Local Energy Action Program.

Project Coordinator for the **Library Automation Publicity**, a media campaign for the Meriam Library, CSU, Chico.

Awards

First Place Award, Women in Communications regional contest for the presentation **The Bauhaus.**

Dean's Award 1980 for the presentation **Learning to See.**

Center for Information and Communications Studies Outstanding Instructional Technologist for the year 1980.

Activities

Member of Women in Communications

Traveled extensively in Asia and Australia

References available upon request
Portfolio available

Design: Sherry Bussey
Type: Olive Antique
Ink: Gray
Paper: White Skytone Text, 70 lb.

ORIGINAL EFFERVESCENT PAIN RELIEVER & ANTACID

Al-Kawashima ®

BRAND

For UPSET STOMACH with HEAD-ACHE or BODY ACHES and PAINS

WITH Visual Communication

For quick relief of UPSET STOMACH, ACID INDIGESTION, or HEARTBURN with HEADACHE or BODY ACHES and PAINS. Especially recommended for these symptoms generally caused by those common GRAPHIC DESIGN PROBLEMS. Pain relief alone: headache or body aches and pains. Fever and muscular aches that may accompany an account.

CAUTION: For best results AL KAWASHIMA works best if stored in a cool/dry place (well lighted). approximately 70°F.

ACTIVE INGREDIENTS: BFA, California State University, Long Beach, Graphic Design. 900 mg. Photography, 800 mg. Illustration, 1000 mg. Production (paste-up, stripping, mechanicals, etc.), 200 mg. Lettering, and special active Pain Reliever, Al Kawashima Effervescent.

DIRECTIONS: Take 1 AL KAWASHIMA for relief up to eight to fourteen hours (sometimes longer) a day.

Design: Al Kawashima
Type: Helvetica, Craw Clarendon
Ink: Light Blue, Dark Blue, Red
Paper: White Husky Cover

Resume | **Deborah Elizabeth Eder**

696 Ladera Lane
Santa Barbara, California 93108
(805) 969-6996

Objective	Experience			Education	References	Deborah Elizabeth Eder
Graphic Designer	Forms & Surfaces, Inc. Architectural Manufacturing Company Box 5215 Santa Barbara, California 93108 1980-present Assist the Art Director with production of brochures, office forms and other printed material for the company. Duties include paste-up, layout, type specifying, photocropping. General knowledge of four color printing, brochure design. Free-Lance Graphic Designer for: Castelberg Associates Landscape Architecture Design Santa Barbara, California Drafting base plans, irrigation plans, planting plans, construction and planting	details, cost estimates and office organization. Dames & Moore Engineering Company Santa Barbara, California Paste-up Peter L.H. Thompson and Associates, Ltd. Landscape Architecture Firm Eugene, Oregon Preparation of plans for presentation and office brochure. University of Oregon Publications Department Eugene, Oregon Design of posters, pamphlets, brochures for the University. Paste-up, layout, and general production procedures. Logo for the University.	Oregana Staff University yearbook 1977-1979 Layout, paste-up, sales. Oregon Beer & Wine Distributors Eugene, Oregon Illustration, paste-up and layout. Eugene Voluntary Action Center Eugene, Oregon Pamphlet illustration Symington Limousine Service Eugene, Oregon Logo design Oregon Daily Emerald University of Oregon Newspaper Eugene, Oregon Illustration for advertisements	University of Oregon Eugene, Oregon Baccalaureate degree in Fine Arts 1977-1979 University of Oxford Oxford, England Summer studies in Art History 1978 College of Marin Kentfield, California Undergraduate studies in Fine Arts 1975-1977 Redwood High School Larkspur, California 1971-1975	Mr. Barnaby Conrad, Jr. 8132 Puesta Del Sol Carpinteria, California 93013 Mrs. Linda Burnham Overby 407 State Street Santa Barbara, California 93101 Mrs. Sydney Baumgartner 113 Mesa Lane Santa Barbara, California 93104	696 Ladera Lane Santa Barbara, California 93108 (805) 969-6996

Design: Deborah Eder
Type: Helvetica
Ink: Red
Paper: White Strathmore Cover

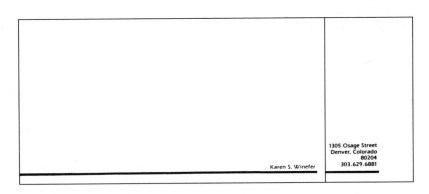

Karen S. Winefer

1305 Osage Street
Denver, Colorado
80204
303.629.6881

Education
1984
Bachelor of Arts Degree
in Graphic Design
California State University,
Chico
   Environmental Graphics
   Lettering
   Typography
   Computer Graphics
   Advertising Design
   Kinegraphics
Minor Emphasis:
Printing Technology
and Marketing
   Copy Preparation
   Technical Drawing
   Screen Printing
   Process Camera Techniques
   Marketing
   Advertising

Experience
1.84/5.84
Freelance Designer
Advertising Campaign
Planner
WestAir Commuter Airlines
Chico, CA.

1.84/5.84
Freelance Designer
Construction Management
California State University,
Chico

1.84/5.84
Advertising Designer
Orion - Campus Newspaper
California State University,
Chico

5.83/8.83
Production Designer
Stuart Graphics
San Ramon, CA.

5.82/8.82
Package Handling
Eastman Kodak Company
San Ramon, CA.

7.80/12.81
Revenue Accountant
World Airways Inc.
Oakland, CA.

Awards and Distinctions
1983
First place
City of San Ramon
Logo Contest

1982
Display
at San Francisco Examiner
Bay to Breakers
T-shirt contest

1980
First Place
Pacific Gas and Electric
Energy conservation
Poster contest

Memberships
1981/84
Designers in Progress
Chico

1983/84
Women in Communications
Chico

1979/84
Sigma Kappa Sorority
Delta Iota Chapter, Chico

1305 Osage Street
Denver, Colorado
80204
303.629.6881

Design: Karen Winefer
Type: Eras, Univers
Ink: Black, Red
Paper: White Strathmore Cover

LINDA CLARK JOHNSON

1073 Serrano Court
Lafayette, CA 94549

415.284.4516

WORK EXPERIENCE	EDUCATION	INTERNSHIPS	AWARDS	MEMBERSHIPS
1983 ▶ GRAPHIC DESIGNER Clark Design & Illustration Chico, CA 1982 to 1983 Consulting graphic designer and illustrator for university, public relations firm, corporations, and other design studios. ▶ LITHOGRAPHIC STRIPPER Quadco Printing, Inc. Chico, CA 1978 to 1983 Responsible for all complex film assembly, including four color process, in quality commercial printing company. Also worked in paste-up, camera, proofing, and platemaking departments.	▶	▶	▶ ANNUAL DESIGN SHOW California State University Chico, CA 1983 Honor Award: Calligraphy	▶ ART DIRECTORS & ARTISTS CLUB Sacramento, CA 1979 to present
1982 ▶	▶ CALIFORNIA STATE UNIVERSITY, CHICO Chico, CA 1979 to 1982 Course work in graphic design; including publication design, corporate identity, typography, illustration, calligraphy, photography, packaging, and creative problem solving.	▶ GRAPHIC DESIGNER Art Department California State University Chico, CA 1981 to 1982 Designed publicity posters for University Art Gallery. ▶ ART DIRECTOR Impulse Magazine California State University Chico, CA 1982 Art direction, scheduling, and quality control for an annual student magazine.	▶ ANNUAL DESIGN SHOW California State University Chico, CA 1982 Best in show: Graphic Design Honor Award: Publication Honor Award: Business System	▶ PRINTING HOUSE CRAFTSMEN'S CLUB Chico, CA 1979 to 1982 Board of Directors, 1980 Graphic Coordinator, 1980 ▶ DESIGNERS IN PROGRESS California State University Chico, CA 1979 to 1982 Steering Committee, 1980
1981 ▶ ILLUSTRATOR CAMERA OPERATOR Chico News & Review Chico, CA 1981 Illustrated and designed editorial sections in weekly community news magazine. Operated horizontal copy camera.	▶	▶ PRODUCTION ARTIST Reber, Glenn, & Marz, Adv. Reno, NV 1981 Designed, specified type, and produced camera ready artwork as full time intern.		
1980 ▶ PRODUCTION ARTIST DesignWare, Inc. San Francisco, CA 1980 Worked as a member of production team for SRA Associates textbook/workbook ''Computer Discovery''				
1979 ▶	▶ CALIFORNIA STATE UNIVERSITY, CHICO Chico, CA 1974 to 1979 B.A. Degree in Fine Arts, emphasis in drawing and watercolor. Graduated with Academic Distinction.		REFERENCES AVAILABLE	

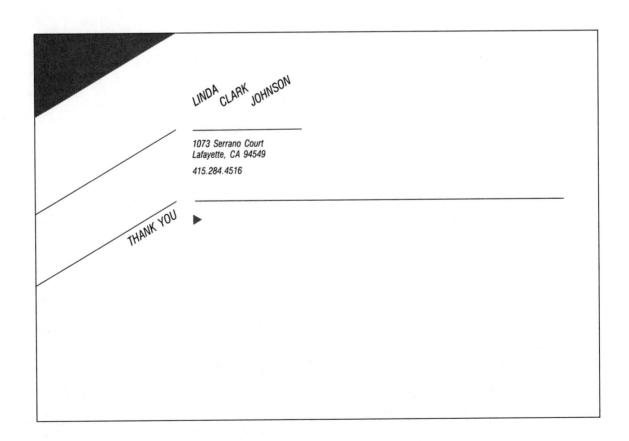

LINDA CLARK JOHNSON

1073 Serrano Court
Lafayette, CA 94549

415.284.4516

REFERENCES

▶ GREGG BERRYMAN
California State University
Chico, CA
916.895.6872, 916.343.6500

▶ GEORGE TURNBULL
    RAE TURNBULL
California State University
Chico, CA
916.895.4308, 916.865.5920

▶ MARILYN WARRENS
Warrens Public Relations
Chico, CA
916.345.7673

▶ RICHARD BRAAK
Quadco Printing, Inc.
Chico, CA
916.894.4061

▶ JAY HALBERT
Shastan, Inc.
Chico, CA
916.894.2027

LINDA CLARK JOHNSON

1073 Serrano Court
Lafayette, CA 94549

415.284.4516

THANK YOU ▶

Design: Linda Clark Johnson
Type: Helvetica
Ink: Gray, Yellow, Varnish
Paper: White Karma Cover

David Sherrod

education:
Art Center College of Design, Pasadena, Ca., 1976-1977
California State University at Sacramento 1972-1974 BA–ART, minor—commercial art
Butte College, Durham, Ca., 1969-1971

affiliations:
1976-1978 ADLA, Art Directors Club of Los Angeles, Society of Illustrators of Los Angeles

personal:
Age 33, normal, healthy and unavailable for the draft

client history:
TRW magazine
Motor Trend magazine
Car Craft magazine
Hot Rod magazine
Skin Diver magazine
Let's Live magazine

Sundancer magazine
Bowmar Publishing – children's books
Diawa Inc.
Lowries Restaurant Corp.
Transcon Truck Lines
Global Marine International
Maxon Industrials
International Aluminum
May Co. Stores
Bullock's Stores

experience:
1/76-Present Freelance Illustration
1/78-6/78 Part-time Instructor, Art Center, College of Design, Pasadena, Ca.
7/74-10/75 Designer Illustrator, Dept. of Parks and Recreation, State of California

Design: David Sherrod
Illustration: David Sherrod
Type: Univers
Ink: Black
Paper: Karma Natural, 80 lb.

R E S U M E

Tom Hermansen   2045 South McClintock Drive #230   Tempe, Arizona 85282   Phone 602-967-3163 + 602-965-3734

E D U C A T I O N

1981   Master of Arts—Public Communication (Graphic Design)
California State University, Chico, California
Corporate identity, publication design, package design,
typography, television graphics, environmental graphics,
advertising, graphic arts, illustration + photography

1975   Standard Secondary Teaching Credential—Art Education
California State University, Hayward, California

1972   Bachelor of Arts—Fine Art
University of California, Davis, California

1970   Associate of Arts—Fine Art
Diablo Valley College, Pleasant Hill, California

Born: August 8, 1950
Marital Status: Single

E M P L O Y M E N T

1980-   Visiting Lecturer, Graphic Design
Illustration, typography,
graphic design, reproduction
design, + portfolio preparation
Arizona State University
Tempe, Arizona

1980   Instructor, Graphic Design
Copy preparation + typography
California State University
Chico, California

1979   Instructor, Graphic Design
Copy Preparation
California State University
Chico, California

1979   Graphic Designer
Image Group Design Studio
Chico, California

1978   Teaching Assistant, Graphic Design
Foundation design class
California State University
Chico, California

1978   Graphics + Darkroom Technician
Duplicating Center
California State University
Chico, California

1976   Teaching Assistant, Graphic Arts
Foundation class
Chabot College
Hayward, California

1975-   Art Director + Designer
1977   Media Services
Chabot College
Hayward, California

1975   Signs + Display
Cost Plus Imports
Walnut Creek + Oakland,
California

1975   Substitute Teacher, Art
San Francisco Bay Area

1975   Summer School Teacher, Arts + Crafts
Mount Eden High School
Hayward, California

1973-   Free-lance Graphic Designer
Logos, stationery systems, signs,
corporate identity, advertising,
architectural graphics, brochures,
package design + illustration

W O R K S H O P S

1979   Illustrators Workshop—California State University, Sacramento, California
1977   Photo + Sound Company, Slide/Tape Workshop—San Francisco, California
1976   Kodak PMT + Plate-making Workshop—San Francisco, California
1973   Nikon School of Photography—San Jose, California
1973   Jade Fon Woo, A.W.S., Watercolor Workshop—Asilomar, California

A W A R D S + S H O W S

1981   School of Art Faculty Show
Arizona State University
Tempe, Arizona

1980   School of Art Faculty Show
Arizona State University
Tempe, Arizona

1978   C.I.C.S. Student Show
"Best in Show"—Graphic Design
California State University
Chico, California

1978   Envision IV Design Conference
Honor Award—Graphic Design
University of California
Davis, California

1965   Eagle Scout Award—Troop 212
Boy Scouts of America
Moraga, California

M E M B E R S H I P S

Art Directors + Artists Club—Sacramento, California
Phoenix Art Directors Club—Phoenix, Arizona
Center for Design—Palo Alto, California

I N T E R E S T S

Calligraphy
Guitar
Photography

References will be furnished upon request

123

Design: Tom Hermansen
Type: Glaser Stencil, Helvetica
Ink: Maroon
Paper: White Vintage Suede. 70 lb.

EXPERIENCE

Assistant Art Director
*Cycle Magazine
Ziff-Davis Publishing Co.
June 1980 to present
Position includes graphic
design and production of
monthly magazine; type
spec editorial matter;
assign, direct and coordinate
freelance photography
and illustration;
prepare mechanicals;
direct studio and
location photography*

Art Director Annuals
*Ziff-Davis Publishing Co.
Full responsibility for graphic
design and production of
two annual publications
including cover design
and photography*

Design Consultant
*D. Randy and Associates
Laguna Beach, CA
Freelance 1980*

Graphic Designer
*Chico News & Review
Chico, CA, 1978-1979
Position included client
consultation and responsibility
for advertising design*

EDUCATION

Bachelor of Arts
*Visual Communications
California State University,
Chico, 1980*

Associate Arts
*Liberal Studies
Moorpark College 1976*

AWARDS

*1979 Pacific Gas & Electric
Energy Conservation
Logo Competition.
Two cash awards.*

Memberships
*The Communication
Arts Society
Art Directors and Artists'
Club of Sacramento*

Thomas J. Saputo

*38 Sandra Court
Newbury Park, CA 91320*

*805/498-3229
References upon request*

Design: Tom Saputo
Type: Optima
Ink: Black
Paper: Gray Classic Linen, 24 lb.

Chēē · kă · să · wă

Patricia Oji Chikasawa

711 Camino Way
Woodland, CA 95695
Work: (916) 448-1227
Home: (916) 666-6834

Work Experience:

Page Design, Inc.
Sacramento, CA
Graphic Design Studio
January 1981 to present

*Design and production of business systems, logos, ads,
fliers, product sheets, brochures, publications, catalogues
and ad campaigns. Work with professionals in related
fields, i.e., photographers, typesetters, printers, copywriters
and color separators, which involves art direction of
photo sessions and supervision of printing. Edit copy,
meet with clients and vendors, and manage studio operations in Mr. Page's absence.*

Representative Clients:

BDN Corporation
California Grocers Association
Excalibur Products
L&M Golf Company, Inc.
McClelland & McNally Advertising Agency
Mercy Hospitals/Mercy Health Care Organization

Education:

California State University, Chico
Graphic Design, Graduate Program

California State University, Fresno
Bachelor of Science Degree
Business Administration

Continuing Education:

Art Directors & Artists Club of Sacramento
(ADAC) Programs
Business of Design Conferences (ADAC)
Envision Conferences (ADAC)
University of California, Davis Extension Program

Free-lance Projects:

Art Directors & Artists Club of Sacramento
CN Power Systems
Country Oaks Racquet Club
George Aoki Farms, Inc.
Golden State Tractor Company
Life Guards, U.C. Davis Recreation Pool
Special Kids of Yolo
Woodland Diesel
Woodland Opera House

References Upon Request

Design: Patti Chickasawa
Type: Optima, Garamond
Ink: Blue
Paper: White Cranes Crest, 28 lb.

Resume:

Gaye L. Graves
1117 Downing Ave.
Chico, CA 95926

Home: (916) 342-6155
Message: (415) 355-3154

Education:

1978—Present
California State University, Chico. Graduate studies in Visual Communications (Graphics). Emphasis on publications, corporate identity, environmental signage, TV graphics, copywriting, and creative problem solving. Soon to complete Masters Program in Instructional Technology. Emphasis on TV, slide-show, film, and audio production. Additional courses in Content Analysis/Learner Needs, Developing Behavioral Objectives, Sequential Content and Learning Tasks, Media Selection Processes, Evaluation of Content/ Product, Design of Instructional Systems.

1971—1975
University of California, Davis. B.S. in Design, with graphic design emphasis.

Employment:

1978—1980
CSUC, Instructional Media Center, graphic designer. Design and production of posters, brochures, TV graphics and other visual instructional aids for the university.

1978
Quadco (printers), graphic production, camerawork, image assembly, platemaking.

1977
Comco
(The Communications Company), production manager, graphics department. Supervised employees, scheduled and produced brochures, posters, magazines, and tabloid newspapers.

1976
State Department of Parks and Recreation (Exhibit Lab). Graphic production of historical exhibits. Duties included exterior signage design, silk screening, repro-camera operation.

1975
CSUS, Center for Instructional Media. Student assistant in graphics department. Designed and produced graphics for instructors and the Media Production Team.

Internships, Activities:

CSUC, Instructional Media Center,
State Department of Parks and Recreation, Exhibit Lab,
CSUS, Center for Instructional Media

Membership in Sacramento Art Directors and Artists Club, Western Art Directors Club, University and College Designers Association, and the Center for Design. Exhibited in CSUC Student Show and the Sacramento Women in Advertising Show.

References furnished upon request.

Design: Gaye Graves
Type: Lubalin Graph
Ink: Brick Red
Paper: White Carrara, 70 lb.

Ronald Fritz-Zavacki

Personal Information
Born 3-20-52/Chicago, IL
Married, no children
Education
University of Illinois
Champaign-Urbana, IL
BFA Graphic Design, May, 1975
BFA Industrial Design, May, 1975
Experience
Design Director
ComUnigraph Incorporated
530 South Grand West
Springfield, IL 62704
Phone 217-544-3737
June, 1977 to present
Designer
University Graphics, Incorporated
Carbondale, IL
August, 1976 to May, 1977
Design Coordinator
Locally Directed Evaluation Project
University of Illinois
August, 1974 to July, 1976
Scope
Corporate Identity,
Publications, Annual Reports,
Marketing Campaigns,
and Exhibits
For
Government,
Health Care, Financial,
Industrial/Manufacturing,
Education, and Service-
oriented clientele
References available
upon request

127

Design: Ron Fritz-Zavacki
Type: Helvetica
Ink: Black
Paper: Tan Classic Linen, 24 lb.

Anne Marie Sheehan

4066 Gresham Avenue Apt. B
San Diego, California 92109
714 272-8312

Professional Experience

81   Patrick Maddux & Company, San Diego, California
       Graphic Designer

Responsibilities
project planning, graphic design, signage, production of
presentations, mechanicals and coordination of related services:
typesetting, printing and photography

Clients/Projects
Carlsbad Research Center, Carlsbad, California
logotype, signage graphics, stationery program

Lawrance Contemporary Furniture, San Diego, California
logotype, store and vehicle identification

Ruhnau, Evans, Ruhnau Architects, Carlsbad, California
site signage

Robert Phillips Company, Costa Mesa, California
logotype, stationery program, clothing labels, brochure

Maintenance Warehouse, San Diego, California
package design, catalog layout

Centerside Office Building, San Diego, California
signage graphics

80   vanDoorn Design, Chico, California
       Graphic Designer

Responsibilities
conceptual and comprehensive design, production

Clients/Projects
Butte County Rice Growers Association, Chico, California
symbol

Nantucket Quilt Store, Chico, California
assistant in design and production of annual catalog

Solar Systems, Chico, California
vehicle identification

Chico First, Chico, California
promotional brochure

80   Chico News & Review, Chico, California
       Graphic Designer

Responsibilities
advertising design and production, client meetings, promotional and
marketing material, use of PMT camera, Compugraphic headliner and
AM Varityper 4510

Academic Experience

80   Internship
       Sacramento Magazine, Sacramento, California
advertising design and production

79   Internship
       Matt Thompson Design, Santa Rosa, California
design and production of symbol for financial planning
company, logotype for condominium development, assisted
layout and production of bi-monthly trade magazine.

77   Internship
       Instructional Media Center, Chico, California
design and production of University materials, coordination of
related services: typesetting, printing and photography

Education

80   California State University, Chico
Bachelor of Arts Degree, Visual Communications

Awards Memberships

79   Sacramento Women in Advertising Student Competition
Best in Show

79   California State University, Chico Student Competition
Honor Award

79-80   California State University, Chico
Designers in Progress

78-80   Sacramento Art Directors and Artists Club

Design: Anne Marie Morgante
Type: Univers
Ink: Black, Red
Paper: Gray Strathmore Writing, 24 lb.

South Van Ness

Opened a design studio dedicated to the fine art of details and problem solving. Clients include Macys, Fairmont Hotels, Pischoff Company and Sierra Club.

San Francisco

Macys California
Staff designer with group that is responsible for in-store graphic design for 21 stores in Northern California and Nevada. Signing needs for all stores was my major area of responsibility. This entailed working drawings, material specs, project coordination, vendor procurement, and site plans for signing projects. Other projects ranged from logos and labels to packages and posters.

Paris

Michel Clave Design
Worked on a freelance basis in this design studio. Did design development and production on various accounts which included:

UFO Jeans of Italy
exterior store graphics

Gervais Yogurt
package

Minhail Hotels
identity

Institut de Louis Pasteur
newsletter

Durham

University of New Hampshire
University Publications
Staff designer in an office that employed six writers and three designers. We handled diverse design and writing needs for the University community. Catalogs, art gallery brochures, theater posters, recruitment flyers, development campaigns, and alumni publications were the type of design problems in which I was involved. Also taught beginning Graphic Design at the University.

Chico

California State University, Chico
BA/Graphic Design
My last year of school was spent working with the University design studio as an intern handling projects from conception through production. Education included extensive French study, computer graphics, photography, typography, packaging, corporate identity, filmmaking, environmental graphics and signing.

1982
1981
1980
1979
1978
1977
1976
1975

129

Design: Brian Collentine
Type: Bodoni
Ink: Black
Paper: White Kromekote, 8 pt.

Noah Nickerson

335½ Heliotrope Drive
Los Angeles, California 90004

213 664 4179

Objective: A position of Art Director which offers growth and design challenges.

Employment:

Industrial Design Affil.
213 878 8080

Answerex Inc.
Advertising

Beverly Hills Office Supply
Logo

Bernard Hodes Adv.
213 487 5990

MacDonald/Douglas
Advertising

Ford Aeronutronics
Advertising

Charles Reilly Co.
213 796 7168

Valley Presbyterian Hospital
'78 Annual Report ('75, '76, '77)

Glendale Memorial Hospital
'78 Annual Report

Charles Reilly Co.
Corporate Identification

Saul Bass & Assoc.
213 466 9701

ITT
Comps

Howard Toboco & Assoc.
213 553 9418

Westdale Savings & Loan
Corporate Identification

Richard Runyan Design
213 879 1999

Orowheat
Packaging

National Semiconductors
Packaging

Bubble-Up
Packaging

Scandiline Industries, Inc.
213 537 6411

Art Director
Advertising/Design

William Mercer, Inc.
213 380 1600

Hughes Airwest
Benefits Manual

TRW
Corporate Manual

Northrop Insurance
Insurance Mailer

Community Redevelopment Agency, C.R.A. (L.A. County)
213 724 6490 Ext. 333

"The People Mover"
Slide and Wall Presentation

Saul Bass & Assoc.
213 466 9701

American Chicle
Presentation Preparation

Lawry's Foods, Inc.
Various Jobs

ITT
Exhibit Graphics

Graphics People, Inc. (Defunct)
213 885 1146

Art Director/Designer

Charles Reilly Co.
213 796 7168

Sierra Bonita Towers
Logo and Brochures

Parke Realty
213 660 8500

Parke Realty
Corporate Identification

Los Angeles City Colleges
213 663 9141 Ext. 24

Slide Teaching Aid

Lealand Scott Design
213 747 9474

BEHR Oil Corporation
Logo Type

Chuck Ax & Staff, Inc.
305 920 5111

Art Director/Vice President

Shield Pacific, Inc.
Concrete & Concrete Products
Kailua Kona, Hawaii 96734

Plant Manager

Port O'Call Delicatessen & Kona Gourmet
Kailua Kona, Hawaii 96734

Manager
Two Locations

Education:

Art Center College of Design
Los Angeles, California

Advertising Design
Admitted with Advanced Standing

Broward Community College
Hollywood, Florida

Humanities

Art Institute of Fort Lauderdale
Fort Lauderdale, Florida

Advertising Design
Student Body President; Initiated
Newspaper and Student Fund
which still exist; worked full time;
Graduated First in the Class.

Central Texas College
Kileen, Texas

Art
Three Dimensional

Missouri University
Columbia, Missouri

Humanities

Central Missouri State College
Warrensburg, Missouri

Small Business/Speech
Human Relations

Received two six-month full scholarships
to Kansas City Art Institute from
High School.

Personal:

Born: May 19, 1945, Salt Lake City, Utah
Marital: Divorced
Health: Excellent

References:

Chuck Ax   305 920 5111
Retired:
Creative Director
N. W. Ayer, New York

Richard MacDonald   404 881 0212
Illustrator

Robert K. Christenberry   904 638 4522
Retired:
Postmaster General
New York

Design: Noah Nickerson
Type: Helvetica
Ink: Gray, Black
Paper: White Gilbert Bond, 24 lb.

Ronald H. Yates

204-C South Ohio Street
Anaheim, California 92805
Telephone:
714/774-3328

OBJECTIVE

Involvement in the visual environment of our professional and educational community through the practice of the communications arts and their related disciplines.

QUALIFICATIONS

Communications arts specialist with agency, publication and design studio experience. Multi-level teaching experience in advertising, art, graphic design and instructional media.

DESIGN PRACTICE

Art Director, Harte-Hanks Communications, Garden Grove, CA
Responsibility includes development and supervision of in-house agency art department. Involvement includes planning, development, design and production of corporate identity programs, print advertising, audio-visual/television production and all sales aids and collateral material.

Other responsibilities include new product planning, design and production, including package design, P.O.P. and sales presentations. Also responsible for purchase of capitol equipment and ancillary supplies.

Assistant Graphics Manager,
J.L.M. Company, Irvine, CA
While at JLM I worked directly with the vice-president of sales and marketing in incentive program development. My responsibilities included premium research, promotion design and production, print advertising and direct mail.

Other duties included photography, A.V. and sales presentations and purchase of printing, advertising specialties and related vendor services.

Freelance Design, Anaheim, CA
During this time I was involved in advertising design, identity programs and real estate advertising programs for Eyedeas Design Group. In addition, I was with CBS Consumer Publications in the production of *SEA* Magazine doing page layout, illustration and production. Also during this time I designed the frontispiece for the book *"50 Golden Years of Oscar"* under the auspices of the Academy of Motion Picture Arts and Sciences.

Account Executive/Partner, Image Group, Chico, CA
While with the Image Group I was responsible for advertising and market research, interfaced with client and media concerning campaign proposals and media purchase. Assisted in conceptual design and production of all two and three dimensional media.

Art Director, *Motorsports Illustrated,* San Jose, CA
During the period that this publication was in print I prepared copy, page layouts, illustrations, photography and final art production. Other duties included ad layout and production and liaison with the printer in production of the magazine.

Assistant Publications Officer,
University of California, Davis, CA
Areas of responsibility included design of official publications, brochures, alumni promotional programs, curricular materials, graduate school bulletins and annual registration catalogs. I also functioned as intra-departmental liaison concerning printing needs, policy and budgets and was a member of the state-wide publications committee.

EDUCATIONAL PRACTICE

Instructor, Extended Day, Cypress College, Cypress, CA
As a member of the Fine Arts department, I am involved in the evening program teaching Basic and Advanced Advertising Design and Advertising Production classes. Curriculum emphasizes typography, design skills, layout techniques and principles of print production through projects planned to provide experience in the graphic design process.

Instructor, International House, London, England
Participant in an intern program teaching English to non-English speaking students. Techniques included audio-visual aids, television, language labs and preparation of instructional materials.

Consultant, Riyadh University, Riyadh, Saudi Arabia
Co-directed T.V. production, graphics and visual aids courses. Designed and produced English as a second language media packages for the College of Medicine. On special assignment I designed a basic media center to be developed at the University of Petroleum and Minerals at Dhahran. Also produced an exhibit of drawings, photographs and prints for the United States Information Service Facility in Riyadh.

Instructor, Butte College, Oroville, CA
Associated with the Business and Art departments, I taught basic advertising and beginning drawing. I organized and directed an advertising workshop for students to gain practical experience in the promotion of school activities through college and local media.

Instructor, California State University, Chico, CA
Taught basic graphic design course within the department of Industry and Technology. Co-directed annual student photography and graphic design exhibit.

EDUCATION

Certificate, Teaching English as a Foreign Language: International Teacher Training Institute, London, England, 1976.

M.A., Visual Communications, California State University, Chico. Interdisciplinary degree of personal design that included the disciplines of Industrial Technology and Mass Communications. The thesis option outline of this program is now part of the master of arts program offered by the Center for Information and Communications Studies, C.S.U., Chico. Thesis: The Modular Photo and the Color of Racing Techniques Imagery. 1974.

B.A., Art Education, California State University, Chico, CA. 1962. Diversified program of study between departments of art and industrial technology. Extracurricular activities included intramural sports, student government and fraternity. Editorial positions on campus publications.

ACTIVITIES

In addition to the foregoing experience, my work has won awards in exhibition, is in private collections here and abroad and has appeared in numerous publications. Other activities and off hour interests include photography, illustration, travel and auto racing as a photographic art form.

Design: Ron Yates
Type: Helvetica
Ink: Black
Paper: Gray Rhododendron Cover

Resume

Abbi Stone
432 Ruthven Avenue
Palo Alto, CA. 94301
(415) 328-7887

1980–Present—Graphic designer
Lawrence Bender & Associates, Palo Alto, CA.
Responsibilities include concept development and design, client
and supplier consultation, and preparation of comprehensive
presentations and camera-ready art.

1980—Freelance graphic designer
Russell Leong Design, Palo Alto, CA.
Responsibilities included production of camera-ready art and
comprehensives, and client consultation.

1978–1979—Graphic designer
California State University, Chico Graphics Studio, Chico, CA.
Responsibilities included concept development and design,
preparation of camera-ready art, client consultation, and supervision of student interns.

1976–1978—Properties manager
California State University, Chico Speech/Drama Department
Responsibilities included poster design and production, construc-
tion of stage sets and props, and supervision of stage crews.

1974–1979—Bachelor of Arts, Art
California State University, Chico
Studies included visual communications, corporate identity, packaging,
drawing, and painting.

References available
on request

Design: Abbi Stone
Type: Stymie
Ink: Brick Red
Paper: Karma Natural, 80 lb.

Graphic Design
Visual Communications
Photography

203 446 6690

Lance Westin
22 East Holly Street
New Haven CT 06522

9/77 . 5/79
Yale University, New Haven CT
typography. drawing oriented design, color, photography, book
design, letterform design, bookbinding, magazine/publication design
MFA 1979
Alvin Eisenman, Paul Rand, Norman Ives, Armin Hofmann, Herbert Matter,
Bradbury Thompson. Alan Fletcher, Andre Gurtler, Inge Druckrey, Christopher
Pullman
Graphic Design
academic courses in geology. natural resources, archaeology

10/76 . 9/77
University of Massachusetts, Boston MA
university released publications. audiovisual/video graphics, environmental
graphics
Visual Information Designer

5/76 . 9/76
Benjamin Thompson+Associates, Cambridge MA
environmental graphics
Graphic Designer

9/72 . 5/76
Yale University, New Haven CT
drawing. design. printmaking, photography, typography, color
BA 1976
academic courses in mathematics, psychology, anthropology, sociology,
classical civilization
Art

2/55
born, Philadelphia PA

references available upon request

133

Design: Lance Westin
Type: Helvetica
Ink: Blue
Paper: Gray Strathmore Bond, 24 lb.

Résumé

Kathy Gard

1524 Bonita Avenue
Mountain View
California 94040
USA

415 961 1329

Career Objective

A design management position which offers creative problem solving and art direction within the marketing department of an international corporation.

Employment

1977–Present	**Graphics Art Director** General Systems Division Hewlett Packard Cupertino, California	Responsibilities include design management, project coordination, art direction of design and production, financial management, management of graphics design staff, vendor communications, interfacing with and designing for HP's international marketing functions.
	Business computers	Experience in the design of international sales literature, literature guidelines for international usage, collateral literature, 35mm marketing slide presentations, publications, retail packaging, and other areas of corporate visual communications including signage, posters, and exhibits.
		Instrumental in standardizing 35mm marketing slide presentations, upgrading creativity and quality of international sales literature, and specifying literature design standards.
1974–1976	**Senior Graphics Designer** Advanced Products Division Hewlett Packard Cupertino, California	Responsibilities included conceptual design, design direction and production.
	Hand-held calculators	Experience in the design of retail packaging, photography, point of purchase displays, owners handbooks, and sales literature.
1972–1974	**Graphics Designer** American Greetings Corp. Cleveland, Ohio	Responsibilities included conceptual design and design production.
	Gift products	Experience in the design of non-greeting card products such as soap, jewelry, leather goods. Also packaging, sales literature, photo art direction, exhibits and collateral material.
1971–1972	**Graphics Designer** The May Company Advertising Department Cleveland, Ohio	Responsibilities included concept studies and design. Experience in the design of special events posters, menus, walk-away promotionals, newspaper layouts and collateral material.

Education

1967–1971	Awarded scholarship to Bowling Green State University, Bowling Green, Ohio. Earned Bachelor of Fine Arts degree with graphic design major.

Professional Activities

Member	1971–Present	Delta Phi Delta, National Art Honorary
	1979–1980	San Francisco Women In Design/Board of Directors
	1978–1980	Peninsula Professional Women's Network
	1978–1980	Sacramento Art Directors and Artists Club
	1980	Palo Alto Western Art Directors Club
	1979–1980	San Francisco Women's Success Teams

Attended	1975, 1979	Aspen International Design Conference
	1979	Sacramento ADAC Illustrators' Workshop
	1977, 1978, 1979	Sacramento ADAC Envision Design Conference
	1977–Present	Hewlett-Packard's Management Development Training Program including wage and salary administration, problem solving and decision making, performance evaluation, managing inter-personal relationships, motivation and communication, time management, affirmative action, effective presentations, practical negotiating skills, stress management, assertiveness management, and non-technical computer class.

Awards	1973	Cleveland Second Annual Art Directors' Show
		Creativity 2 Annual Review
	1974	Cleveland Third Annual Art Directors' Show
		Creativity 3 Annual Review

| Recognition | 1979 | Selection for Women In Design national travelling portfolio |
| | 1980 | Featured exhibitor of *West Week '80*, Los Angeles, Design Seminar |

Personal

| Birth | 1949 | Ravenna, Ohio |
| Interests | | Photography, design, art, travel |

Portfolio available on request.

Design: Kathy Gard
Type: Helvetica
Ink: Gray
Paper: Ivory Kilmory, 80 lb.

**Donald Price
Resume**

**Graphic Design
Photography**

3400 I Street
Sacramento, CA 95816
916 444-3490

Work Experience

Principal Partner
Powell and Price
Sacramento, CA

January 1977 to Present
Clients include Taylor Development, Feather River Bank, Federal Projects, Inc., along with a number of local and regional businesses

Art Director
The Bennitt Group
Sacramento, CA

January 1975 to December 1977
Clients include Sacramento Convention Center, Buffalo Beer Distributors, Far West Forests. Sacramento Savings and Loan, California State Library

Staff Designer
Industrial Design Affiliates
Beverly Hills, CA

September 1974 to December 1975
Clients include Technicolor Inc., Airstream Trailers Inc., Rockwell Int.

Contract Photographer
California State Fair, 1974
Sacramento, CA

July 1974 to September 1974
Headed a team of photographers that photographed for promotions, press releases, and recording of events and people that participated in the fair activities; extensive relations with the public, dignitaries, UPI and AP

Freelance Design/Photography
Image Group
Chico, CA

1974 - 1975
Advertising layouts, comprehensive art, promotional photography

Design/Photography
Studios Graphik
Chico, CA

1973- 1974
Business identity systems and correspondence, packaging, product and promotional photography

Education

California State University Chico
Chico, CA

June 1974
Graduated with a Bachelor of Arts Degree in Visual Communication. Extensive study in graphic design, photography and television production. Worked with University Relations designing school collateral and instructional media

Photography Laboratory Assistant
Provided assistance and instruction to photography students about equipment and procedures

Shasta Junior College
Redding, CA

Associate of Arts Degree in Fine Arts. Studied Fine Arts and business administration

Military Duty

Captain
US Army Corps of Engineers

June 1968 to January 1972
Received commission from US Army Engineer Officer Candidate School. Held responsible command and staff positions in theaters of operation in the USA, Germany and Vietnam. Honorable discharge

Activities

President
Art Directors and Artists Club
Sacramento, CA

1977-1978
Responsible for the organization of club events dealing with nationally known speakers, activities, workshops, monthly newsletters, and a two day symposium with attendance over 650 people

Travel

Toured Europe, Asia, Mexico, Canada, and Western USA. Photographed sights and graphic design for research and reference

Design: Don Price
Type: Helvetica
Ink: Warm Red, Gray
Paper: Strathmore Bond, 24 lb.

Greg Silveria

1758 London Drive
Benicia
California 94510
Home 707 746-5385
Work 415 956-7575

Education

California State University, Chico, 1973. Bachelor of Science degree in Graphic Communication with a minor in Marketing and Management. Special emphasis in graphic design and photography.

Professional Objectives

Presently employed as a Design Director. Seeking similar responsibilities in a design/management capacity.

Experience

1978 S&O Consultants, San Francisco
Design Director in Corporate Identity and Packaging. Responsible for project management involving client contact, design evaluation, presentation work, budget control and design implementation.

1974 Design and Market Research Laboratory, Santa Clara. Designer and Photographer in Packaging, Corporate Identity and photo studio production of 35mm slide presentations.

Summer 1971-73 Solano County Public Works, Fairfield. Engineers Aide—field representative for resident civil engineer. Duties included construction drafting, survey crew and on-site construction inspection.

Major Design Programs

Anheuser-Busch Companies
Bank of America-Versatel
Chevron Chemical Company
Crocker Bank
First Interstate Bank
Fotomat Corporation
Mrs. Fields Cookies
Omark Industries
Pioneer Bank
Russell Athletic
Transamerica Corporation

Design: Greg Silveria
Type: Avant Garde
Ink: Red, Black
Paper: Gray Strathmore Bond, 24 lb.

Piper Murakami   *800 Lyon Street #3*   *San Francisco, CA 94115*   *415 **922 2421***

Graphic   *D e s i g n e r*

EXPERIENCE

Adams/Murakami
Graphic & Environmental
Design
San Francisco, CA
1/81 - present

Freelance Graphic Designer

Vanderbyl Design
Graphic Designer
San Francisco, CA
2/80 - 8/81

Responsibilities: *Assistant to principal, conceptual and comprehensive design, client and supplier consultation, production coordination for corporate identity, publications, brochures, catalogs, environmental signage.*

Clients: *ASID, California Academy of Sciences, Coldwell Banker Real Estate, Foremost McKesson, Mobil Redwood Shores, Inc., Modern Mode Inc., San Francisco Opera Association.*

Image Group
Graphic Designer
Chico, CA
1/79 - 1/80

Responsibilities: *Conceptual and comprehensive design, art direction, production coordination for corporate identity, magazine publication, brochures, packaging, illustration.*

Clients: *California State University, Chico; Chico Magazine, Chico-San, Inc.; W.S. Knudsen Co.*

**California State
University, Chico**
Alumni Association
Editor/Art Director
11/78 - 5/79

Responsibilities: *Editing, art directing, and designing 1979 Yearbook. Reviving a campus publication which has not been published for 10 years.*

**California State
University, Chico**
Impulse Magazine
Art Director
3/79 -5/78

State of California
Department of Health
Graphic Artist
11/75-12/77

EDUCATION

**California State
University, Chico**
Bachelor of Arts Degree
Visual Communications
5/79

**California State
University, Sacramento**
Major: Communication
studies, art.
Intermittent
through 12/77

**Sacramento City
College**
Associates of Arts Degree
Major: Art
Minor: Graphic Arts
1/76

MEMBERSHIP

American Institue
of Graphic Arts

Art Directors and
Artist Club, Sacramento

AWARDS

Visual Communicator
Award, 1979
California State
University, Chico

Directory Cover
Competition, 1979
Art Directors and
Artist Club, Sacramento

Student Show Honor
Award, 1978
California State
University, Chico

STUDY TOUR

Design and Art Tour:
London/Basel/Paris, 8/79
Visited Pentagram,
Lock/Pettersen, Ltd.,
Ciba-Geigy, Armin Hoffman
and Wolfgang Weingart
at Algemeine Gewerk-
eschule,and major art
museums.

Design: Piper Murakami
Type: Univers
Ink: Black
Paper: White Strathmore Bond, 24 lb.

Kevin James Cahill

D   E   S   I   G   N

500 Lone Pine, Box 801
Bloomfield Hills, Michigan 48013
313 645-3336

R   E   S   U   M   E

E   D   U   C   A   T   I   O   N

Cranbrook Academy of Art
Bloomfield Hills, Michigan
MFA Graphic Design, May 1983

California State University, Chico
BA Visual Communications, May 1981
Minor Cluster: Printing Technology, Film

A   W   A   R   D   S

1981 CSU, Chico Commencement Exercises
Center for Information and Communication Studies
Outstanding Student Award

1981, 1980 CSU, Chico Design/Photography Student Show
Honor Awards, Design and Photography

1977-1981 Graphic Arts Technical Foundation
Raise Foundation Scholarship

P   U   B   L   I   C   A   T   I   O   N   S

Print Regional Design 1982 Annual
Cranbrook Educational Community Annual Report

Publication Design 14
Publication Designers of New York Awards Annual
Editorial spread, Chico News & Review

Editorial Design by Roy Paul Nelson, University of Oregon
Editorial spreads, Chico News & Review

P   R   O   F   E   S   S   I   O   N   A   L

Experience

1981-1983 Design Michigan
Editorial Designer, Design Quarterly

1977-1979 Chico News & Review
Art Director. Developed and maintained format for
weekly newsmagazine, circulation 20,000
Supervised staff of five design and production people

Organizations

ADAC, Art Directors and Artists Club
Sacramento, California
Attended Envision Conferences 4, 5, 6, and 7

Attended International Design Conference
in Aspen, June 1982

R   E   F   E   R   E   N   C   E   S

Katherine McCoy, Co-Chairperson Department of Design
Cranbrook Academy of Art
500 Lone Pine, Box 801, Bloomfield Hills, Michigan 48013
313 642-9570

Jack Williamson, Director Design Michigan
500 Lone Pine, Box 801, Bloomfield Hills, Michigan 48013
313 645-3316

John Gregg Berryman, Associate Professor
Center for Information and Communication Studies
California State University, Chico 95926
916 895-6872

Design: Kevin Cahill
Type: Garamond
Ink: Maroon, Blue-Green
Paper: Ivory Cranes Crest, 28 lb.

Douglas Powell
Design Consultant

Biography

Doug Powell has nearly 10 years experience in the area of corporate identification, communication and planning.

As a consultant, his expertise takes him into the area of "total image planning" with particular emphasis on multi-level identity systems, including trademark and signage systems design.

Prior to becoming a private consultant, Doug held both design management and account management positions with the two largest design/marketing firms in the nation — Landor Associates and S&O Consultants, respectively.

During this time he was responsible for directing all aspects of the First Interstate corporate identity program as well as the recent Transamerica identity modernization.

Doug is a graduate of California State University, Chico with a degree in industrial technology.

Major Project Background

Alex Foods, Inc.
Anheuser-Busch
Bank of America
Criton Corporation
First Interstate Bank
Foster Farms
Harrah's Hotels and Casinos
Holiday Inns, Inc.
Omark Industries
Transamerica

| **Resumé** | Douglas M. Powell | 8721 Seckel Court
Elk Grove, CA 95624
Telephone 916 685-7800 |

| **Education** | California State University, Chico
Chico, California | BA Industrial Technology, 1973
Primary Emphasis in Graphic Design
Secondary Emphasis in English and Business |

| **Certifications** | California Community Colleges
Art, Design and Photography | |

Experience

Present	**Private Consultant** Design/Marketing	Primary services include development of visual communication and marketing programs for corporate clientele.
1979–82	**Account Director** S&O Consultants Inc., San Francisco	General responsibilities include overall planning, development and supervision of corporate identification and consumer packaging programs.
		Holiday Inn brand identification and signing **Bank of America** consumer forms **Alex Foods, Inc.** institutional and retail food packaging **Pliana** brand identity (Mexico) **Transamerica Occidental Life** identity changeover **First Interstate Banks** signage implementation **Nalley's** retail food packaging
	Design Director S&O Consultants Inc., San Francisco	General responsibilities included overall design development and supervision of corporate identification, signage and consumer packaging projects.
		First Interstate Banks corporate identification **Bank of America** computer forms program **Anheuser-Busch** wholesaler catalogue program **Criton Corporation** corporate identification **Omark Industries** retail packaging **Harrah's** corporate identification **Alex Foods, Inc.** institutional food packaging **Transamerica** corporate identification
1978	**Project Director** Landor Associates, San Francisco	General responsibilities included design development and supervision of medium scale corporate identification projects, primarily in South and Central America and Italy.
1976–77	**Contract Designer** Ross Design, San Francisco	General responsibilities included design development and implementation of specific corporate promotional programs for Metropolitan Furniture, Robert Long Lighting, The Rucker Corporation, KCBS-FM Radio, and Botsford Ketchum Advertising.
1974–75	**Design Director** Cal Expo, Sacramento	Primary responsibility included the development and implementation of a full scale facility identification and signage program.
1973–74	**Exhibit Coordinator** California State Parks and Recreation, Sacramento	Primary responsibility included the design development and implementation of a comprehensive exhibit program for The Seeley Museum of Transportation, San Diego.

| **Honors and
Publications** | Cree (French)
Graphis Posters, 1977 (Swiss)
The Book of American Trademarks, Vol. 4
The Book of American Trademarks, Vol. 5
Letterheads/1
Communication Arts, Vol. 18, No. 5
World of Logotypes, Vol. II | |

Design: Doug Powell
Type: Helvetica
Ink: Black
Paper: White Strathmore Bond, 24 lb.

Sandra McHenry

	Education	Experience	Personal

78 | **Kent Summer in Switzerland**
Color, drawing and representation, typography, and form | | 27, single and healthy

running |

77 | | |

76 | | **California State University, Chico Instructional Media Center Graphic Designer**
Directed application of University's identity to publications, signage, business forms. Helped develop sub-systems for institutes, grants. Planned type systems for catalogues, new publications, posters. |

75 | **California State University, Chico**
Graduate Program
Film and TV, Drawing, Illustration, Printmaking, Psychology | |

74 | | **Unique Printing**
Graphic Designer
Prepared camera ready art, operated IBM typesetting machine, plate-making machine |

73 | **California State University, Chico**
Graphic Design,
Visual Communications
June 1974 Bachelor of Arts
Packaging, corporate identity, typography, advertising, information systems, photomechanical reproduction, black and white and color photography | **Brock Printing**
Graphic Designer
Prepared camera ready art, typesetting, dealt with special problems of book production |

72 | | | tennis

photography |

71 | | |

70 | | | skiing |

1969 | **Montana State University**
Industrial design, interior design, architecture, graphic design, ceramics, drawing, painting | |

Design: Sandra McHenry
Type: Helvetica
Ink: Red
Paper: White Karma, 80 lb.

Sandra McHenry

	Experience	Education	Awards
81	**Ross Design/ Opus Group** Design and production of corporate identity programs, annual reports, collateral materials, catalogs, books, magazines and advertising. Responsibilities included client contact, press checks, photo art direction, maintenance of production schedules, supervision of other employees.		
80			
79			
78	**Lawrence Bender and Associates** Design and production of annual reports, corporate brochures, corporate magazines and collateral material.	**Kent Summer in Switzerland** Color, drawing and representation, typography, and form	**Communication Arts Society of Los Angeles Certificate of Merit**
77	**California State University, Chico Instructional Media Center** Directed application of University's identity to publications, signage, business forms. Helped develop sub-systems for institutes, grants. Planned type systems for catalogues, new publications, posters. Scripted multi-media program for use in graphic design program.		**UCDA Excellence Award**
76			**California State University Chancellor's Grant Conference for design professionals in the university and college system. Emphasis was placed on the improvement and quality of design as applied to a university's visual communications.**
75		**California State University, Chico Graduate Program** Film and TV, Drawing Illustration, Printmaking, Psychology	**UCDA Excellence Award★★★ UCDA Gold Award**
74	**Unique Printing, Chico** Prepared camera ready art, operated IBM typesetting machine, plate-making machine.	**California State University, Chico Graphic Design Visual Communications June 1974 Bachelor of Arts** Packaging, corporate identity, typography, advertising, information systems, photomechanical reproduction, black and white and color photography	**UCDA Silver Award UCDA Merit Award**
73	**Block Printing, Chico** Prepared camera ready art, typesetting for books, posters, catalogs, brochures.		
72			
71			
70		**Montana State University Industrial Design— Firenze Summer Program** Art History, Industrial Design	
1969		**Montana State University** Industrial design, interior design, architecture, graphic design, ceramics, drawing, painting	

Design: Sandra McHenry
Type: Century Oldstyle, Helvetica
Ink: Gray
Paper: White Strathmore Bond, 28 lb.

Resume
Bibliography

Beyond the Resume.
Herman Holtz.
New York:
McGraw-Hill.

Dress for Success.
John T. Molloy.
New York:
Warner Books, Inc.

How to Put Your Book
Together and Get a Job
In Advertising.
Maxine Paetro.
New York:
Hawthorn Books.

How to Write Better Resumes.
Adele Lewis.
New York:
Barrons.

Marketing Yourself.
The Catalyst Staff.
New York:
Bantam Books.

Resume Writing.
Burdette Bostwick.
New York:
John Wiley & Sons, Inc.

The Perfect Resume.
Tom Jackson.
Garden City, N.Y.:
Anchor Press/Doubleday.

Resumes for Hard Times.
Bob Weinstein.
New York:
Simon and Schuster.

Design
Bibliography

Graphic Design Career Guide.
James Craig.
New York:
Watson-Guptill.

Graphic Designer's
Production Handbook.
Norman Sanders.
New York:
Hastings House.

Graphis Diagrams.
Walter Herdeg.
Zurich:
The Graphic Press.

Graphics Master.
Dean Phillip Lem.
New York:
Art Direction Book Co.

Notes on Graphic Design
and Visual Communication.
Gregg Berryman.
Los Altos, CA:
Crisp Publications, Inc.

Phototypesetting:
A Design Manual.
James Craig.
New York:
Watson Guptill.

Pocket Pal, A Graphic
Arts Production Handbook.
New York:
International Paper Co.

The Complete Guide to
Illustration and Design
Techniques and Materials.
Terence Dalley, ed.
London:
QED Publishing Ltd.

F

A

4

R

R